# THE
# PURPOSE
# FORMULA

## LEARN TO BE FULLY ALIVE

JESSICA RIMMER, PHD

©2025 by Jessica Rimer

Published by hope*books
2217 Matthews Township Pkwy
Suite D302
Matthews, NC 28105
www.hopebooks.com

hope*books is a division of hope*media

Printed in the United States of America

First paperback edition.

Paperback ISBN: 979-8-89185-304-1
Hardcover ISBN: 979-8-89185-155-9
Ebook ISBN: 979-8-89185-156-6
Library of Congress Number: 2025930638

hope*books
hopebooks.com
Because the world needs your hope-filled words now more than ever.

"*The Purpose Formula* is a powerful blend of inspiration and practicality. Jessica Rimmer helps readers uncover their unique purpose with a mix of personal stories, foundational truths, and actionable tools. She reminds us that purpose isn't just about what we achieve; it's about who we become and how we contribute to the world around us. This book is a must-read for anyone ready to step into the life they were created to live."

KEVIN DESHAZO
Author of *Keep Chopping Wood* and *Into the Storm*

"Jessica Rimmer, PhD, is one of the most impactful leaders I know because she not only knows her purpose but lives it out with inspiring authenticity. In *The Purpose Formula*, Jessica offers Christian leaders a practical and empowering framework that helps them and their teams truly flourish. Her wisdom and guidance make this book a must-read for anyone longing to live with greater clarity and intention."

KAT ARMSTRONG
Author of *No More Holding Back* and the *Storyline Bible Study* series
Host of the Holy Curiosity podcast

"*The Purpose Formula* is packed with practical insights, timeless truths, and compelling stories to help you step into a purpose-filled life. Dr. Jessica Rimmer guides you along a pathway to uncover meaning and find redemption for your pain. Embrace these principles, and you will max out on life!"

DAVID SKIDMORE
Founder of LeaderGrowth and Author of *Unstuck*

"Jessica Rimmer has done it. She has created *The Purpose Formula* to be both deep and relevant. If you are longing to solve one of life's mysteries - "what is my purpose?" then buckle up and dive into the depths."

JEREMIE KUBICEK
Wall Street Journal Bestseller
Author of the *5 Voices, Peace Index, 100X Leader,* and others

This book is dedicated to every lonely heart who has wondered if they have a place in this world. To my children, may you explore your purpose with wild abandon and live the adventure that God calls you to. And to my husband, the person who always makes space for me to live my purpose.

# CONTENTS

# PREFACE

This book has likely found its way into the hands of a driven, weary person. Perhaps you are seeking confirmation that you are on the right path. Maybe you are picking up this book because you have felt like you have lived a life wandering. Whatever the reason you chose to read this book, I'm glad we are meeting. I want you to find direction and reception in these pages. Here is what I know: you are not reading this by accident.

For that reason, I want to provide a few notes about what purpose is NOT before we enter a discussion of what yours might be. The reason I find it important to explain what purpose is not is because there are limitations on what purpose can and cannot provide for us. We enter into an exasperating relationship with anything or anyone when we demand what that thing or that person is unable to provide. Healthy relationships require that we accept proper expectations. Your relationship with purpose can only thrive if you know that purpose is a gift, but it is not your ultimate answer to fulfillment. There are two boundaries I would like to propose. These boundaries are intended to set you free from the excruciating pain that comes from asking more of purpose than it can deliver to you.

First, your purpose is not your identity. Meaning you have value and worth regardless of how well you live out your purpose. Second, your purpose is not your job. Sometimes, we do get lucky and are vocationally aligned with a role that is a robust expression of purpose. However, it is not primarily *what* we do; purpose is how we do what we do. It is not a role that we play or a function of vocation alone. It is how we show up and shift an environment, relationship, or outcome. I will unpack each of these boundaries in this preface. Please don't sleep on these concepts. Ensuring that you filter your search for purpose with these guardrails in place will protect your heart from the snares that easily entangle us as we seek to live with meaning.

Purpose does not equal identity. Identity is the state of our being. Identity lays the foundation for a properly understood purpose. While the roles that we play and the values we hold matter, our personhood holds inherent value apart from what we do. I have heard it put this way, "we are human beings, not human doings." That sentiment attempts to communicate that who we ARE is important and valuable apart from what we DO. Said another way, we are accepted and whole, distinct from the work we do. Parents know this innately the first time they hold a newborn baby. That little human has done nothing to deserve affection. In fact, for the birth mother, the child has caused a great deal of suffering. However, the first time a parent locks eyes with that helpless human, love explodes. That baby is a person worth fighting for. This experience is a lot like what it means to be a person with identity value.

A proper biblical understanding of human identity draws its origins from Genesis 1, where God makes man and woman in his own image and pronounces their creation "good." Genesis 1:26, "Then God said, 'Let us make man in our image, in our likeness, and let them rule over the fish of the sea and the birds of the air, over the livestock, and all the earth, and over all the creatures that move along the ground." It is understandable that human identity and the work they are given to do are conflated. However, the slight distinction is chronological. God made man and woman in his image, with a role to play and responsibilities to complete. However, in Genesis 1:31, it says, "God saw all that he had made, and it was very good. And there was evening and there was morning—the sixth day." This proclamation was made upon God's inspection of His handiwork. When God looked at his children, love burst forth. God had completed His work, but mankind had not yet done anything. God proclaimed that human beings had inherent value because of what HE had done. Not because of what they had done.

In case you think I am overemphasizing a tiny distinction, allow me to explain why it is so important that we understand this contrast. If we only live out our purpose when we successfully complete our work, then our identity is threatened by failure to complete our work. Don't get me wrong, our work matters, and I will unpack that in this book. However, our status with the Creator cannot be threatened by human failure. He has declared our existence good. We see in Romans 5:8 that God continues this pattern of working for us and giving us a status we didn't earn. Paul writes, "But God demonstrates his love for us in this: While we were still sinners, Christ died for us." We live out our purpose after the finished work of Christ. God has given his creation a stamp of approval that is irrevocable, non-negotiable, and permanent. He secured our identity as chosen Children. We have value before we do anything. Our purpose is an outworking of our identity. It is not the origin.

Secondly, our purpose is not our job. It is hard for any of us to fully shed the impact of our historical time period. In the 21st century, we place a premium on paid work. I have heard it expressed more than once that a person's salary is a direct reflection of their personal sense of value. Throughout history, work has taken on many forms, paid and unpaid. Even now, unpaid workers who are lifting the responsibilities of a family unit can sometimes feel like they are squandering their lives because there is not a dollar figure attached to the work they do. Often, this relationship between work and value creation can be a temptation to siphon energy into the identity gap that we feel. There is real power in success or in the kinetic energy that comes from creating and ideation in a professional setting. This professional vitality can lead us into an addictive relationship with working.

Purpose is how we approach our jobs, but our jobs are not the key to clarity in our purpose. If we truly have a sense of what our purpose is, it pervades all of our circles of influence. It is how we show up and serve wherever we are. Understanding that purpose is not our job also allows us to escape the victim mentality that can come when we are in difficult work environments. When our sense of purpose is distinct from the environmental conditions, we truly can approach our work and relationships with the mind of Christ. Living with a sense of our true identity intact allows us to approach every day with the eyes of our hearts opened toward hope. Seeking to serve others rather than to be served by the people in front of us.

It took me a while to understand that identity comes first. I have a section of blank pages at the end of my bible. On them, I began to create a list of declarations that the scriptures make about humankind. When I get discouraged and feel like discouragement is biting at my heels, I find the list a comforting review. If you would like to do a little bit of an identity study on what God says about you, I encourage you to check out this sampling:

Because of Christ, we are:

- Chosen, God's special possession, anointed, a declarer of praise, holy (1 Peter 2)

- One who speaks to God (Ephesians 3:12)
- God's workmanship (Ephesians 2:10)
- Priests/Ministers (Isaiah 61:6)
- Someone in whom God delights (Zephaniah 3:17)
- A new creation, Saints (2 Corinthians 5:17)
- Alive in Christ (Ephesians 2:4-5)
- Reconciled to God (Romans 5:10)
- Justified; at peace with God (Romans 5:1)
- Known by God (Galatians 4:9)
- Brought near (Ephesians 2:13)
- Dearly loved children (Ephesians 5:1)

I would love for you to start your own identity list. Anytime you read an identity declaration in scripture, flip to the back of your bible or open a note in your phone. Record the statement and the location. When you are struggling to feel worthy, revisit this list. Our identity is secure in Christ.

Living out our purpose is a reasonable act of worship where we get to act as agents of redemption to bring God's Kingdom to bear in our contemporary experience. Perhaps if we release the pressure of identity value from our pursuit of purpose, we might find a way to get curious and even excited about finding our unique purpose formula. It is never too late to contribute. Regret, after all, is not a kingdom concept. We live in the reality of redemption. He is making all things new. Even your understanding of His intended purpose for you.

# CHAPTER ONE

# PURPOSE

"Now, dear, it isn't the bold things,
Great deeds of valour and might,
That count the most in the summing up of life at the end
of the day.
But it is the doing of old things,
Small acts that are just and right;
And doing them over and over again, no matter what
others say;
In smiling at fate, when you want to cry, and in keeping at
work when you want to play—
Dear, those are the things that count."

Poems of Purpose by Ella Wheeler Wilcox

**P**urpose is defined as the *reason* that something exists. Another way to put it is the intended *objective* of its existence is an object's purpose. These definitions hint at meaning and relevance. Some words that often surround the idea of purpose are calling, mission, significance, goals, and many more. Each of these concepts connect us to the idea that people are created to accomplish something. Many books have been written on the importance of purpose. Nearly 25 years ago, I remember reading the opening lines to *The Purpose Driven Life*, "It's not about you. The purpose of your life is far greater than your personal fulfillment, your peace of mind, or even your happiness." The author goes on to express how we live inside of a divinely woven narrative. The stories of our lives are meaningfully told as a part of the larger story of humanity and God's plan for redemption.

The mere existence of other established works on the topic caused me to ask, *Does the world need another book about purpose? Don't we know by <u>now</u> that life has meaning?* It seems obvious enough that we are here for a reason and our life counts for something. Yet, existential crisis persists for too many. Like generations before us, we find ourselves wrestling with age-old questions of significance. It seems that the human heart is ever on a quest to explain its rhythm. We long to find ourselves part of a symphony rather than a disconnected melody.

Unfortunately, living without a sense of purpose and meaning is a pervasive experience for many people. More than half of young Americans live with a constant feeling of being down, depressed, or even hopeless. When individuals get the sense that their life is purposeless, a common question is, "What's the point of all of this anyway?" This question can trigger a downward spiral. When people get the sense that life lacks meaning, that feeling casts a shadow on relationships, tasks, jobs, and motivation. This experience can lead to boredom, frustration, or anxiety and depression. Sociologist Corey Keyes might refer to this as the in-between state of "languishing" where we are not thriving but we are also not quite depressed. This blah feeling can lead some toward existential crisis while others seem to stay motionless as a means to cope with reality. According to researcher Mihaly Csikszentmihalyi, "Purpose provides activation energy for life." Purposelessness happens when we lack motivation and vigor for life. This book explores how we can activate our energy.

Roughly 25% of Americans experience invigorating energy and report they have a clear sense of purpose. Having a strong sense of purpose is associated with a myriad of benefits, such as a healthier immune system, greater resilience, and a happier mood. Research also demonstrates that the more conscious we are of our purpose, the more likely we are to be happy, create strong relationships, choose healthy habits, and have overall better mental and physical health. In the workplace, employees who have a strong sense of purpose have higher retention and engagement, resulting in better financial outcomes for the business and the individual. "Knowing your purpose strengthens your sense of self; it gives you a way to explain who you are both to other people and to yourself." Self-awareness around purpose is a guiding light for individuals, driving clarity in goals, relationships, career choices, and boundaries. Our purpose clarifies the 'why' in our yeses and nos. Life purpose increases our ability to be intentional throughout our lives.

Purpose gives our life direction and significance. Csikszentmihalyi goes on to write, "One cannot lead a life that is truly excellent without feeling that one belongs to something greater and more permanent than oneself." In other words, purpose is imperative to a fulfilling life. With the benefits of purpose so pronounced and the consequences of purposelessness so clear, it begs the question, why do so many people persist without uncovering their designed purpose? Why do so many people chase success without knowing the fulfillment and clarity that purposeful significance could bring? Why is there such a pervasive experience of meaninglessness in a world where there are so many ways to connect and make a difference?

I know what it is like to struggle with a pervasive sense that something is missing...to stand at the crossroads of desiring more purpose for my life and yet coming up empty-handed. I was not always a wife, mom to three kids, running a business and championing others in their purpose. I remember my first big bout with purposelessness.

It hit me in the early stages of college. Years later, I would come to find out how common the timing is for this existential crisis. When someone transitions from emerging adulthood to college, the question shifts from who they might become to the reality that aimless behavior bears consequences on decisions for the future. I had gone to school with a real sense of calling and goal orientation. However, during my freshman year of college, I began to wrestle with big questions about God and His will in the classroom and faced major gaps in my character and relationships outside the classroom. I no longer looked at myself as someone who could make a difference; rather, when I looked in the mirror, what I saw was a flawed, broken human who may never amount to the dreamy ideals to change the world that led me down this pathway. I was struggling with guilt and shame due to a loss of purpose and some poor moral decisions I was making. A depression spiral resulted, leading to some very real suicidal ideation. I know the pain of hopelessness because I, too, have felt the darkness tempt me to take final control of it.

When we lose our sense of purpose or even our confidence to pursue it, darkness often feels like the most logical ally. It can be hard to put one foot in front of the other and move toward the truth of who we are and the hope of what we are made to do when the weight of despondency descends. While this is not a book on mental health, it does flirt with the concepts because of how tied into our well-being and flourishing it is to have a purpose.

My favorite definition of mental health is "a radical commitment to reality." This comes from John Mark Comer's book, *Live No Lies*, where he discusses the deep importance of truth-telling to living a whole and integrated life. In her book *Dopamine Nation*, Dr. Anna Lembke argues that truth-telling improves our lives. Scientifically, it improves our ability to utilize our executive function that guides healthy decision making. Truth-telling, while painful from time to time, can also be wondrous. The truth about reality is not only the most brutal thing about us, it is also the most glorious. We are not only the worst versions of ourselves, we are also the best versions of ourselves. Our purpose is representative of God's intended best for us. In fact, when He created us, He thought ahead to set us up to actualize that potential.

## You are a Masterpiece

Ephesians 2:10 (CSB) states, "We are his *workmanship*, created in Christ Jesus for good works, which God prepared ahead of time for us to do." Some translations use the word "masterpiece" or "handiwork" instead of workmanship. I love this idea because it makes me picture God as an artist in His workshop rather than as a foreman over an assembly line. He thoughtfully crafted each detail of His design for the purpose He imagined. I envision Him, like a woodworker, concentrating on each turn of the lathe and carefully choosing the colors for our top coat. This verse reveals that not only do we have a designed purpose to do good works, but that we are created with the care and pride of an artist. Our design is suited to serve the good works that are ahead of us.

This passage, while beautiful, can be misconstrued as meaning we are here for what we can do. While there is tangible value in what we do, there is an inherent dilemma in thinking about purpose primarily as an output. Purpose as output communicates that we are primarily valuable because of what we accomplish rather than possessing essential value because of who we are. While objects are definitively aligned with their use, human purpose is deeper and more dynamic. Human purpose goes beyond mere utilitarian thinking of achievement or pragmatic duty. Purpose is our unique design working in harmony with the needs of the world. Purpose could be described as the melody of our lives that drives the sense of satisfaction that our existence is orchestrated for something greater. We understand that we are created with purpose as we see our lives weaving together with the greater story of humanity.

Unlike pragmatic purpose, human purpose is energetic in its impact. Dr. Caroline Leaf, mental health expert and author, writes, "Your purpose is not the thing you do. It is the thing that happens to others when you do what you do." Our purpose should spark life in others. Living our purpose is a contribution we offer to others as we devote our lives to our communities. While human purpose is best expressed in service to others, it also serves the individual providing the service. As we live and serve in our designed purpose, we participate in the joy and meaning that others receive from us. Purpose is a gift. God gave each human a unique purpose to contribute to themselves and to society as a whole. Purpose is always an experience of commingling. Our purpose is intertwined with the loving intent of God and the activity of those around us.

God desires for us to experience the joy of participating in His plan for the world. This means that our purpose is *for* us, but it does not end *with* us. We get to share in the gift of purpose. Straightforwardly, we get to participate in the process. Participatory joy is a distinctive feature of human purpose. God invites us into a discovery process with Him whereby we gain awareness through discovery and experiences, participating in the wonder of unearthing our purpose. This sense of purpose facilitates connection with God and others. In this way, purpose is both personal and mutual.

Imagine Christmas morning. Mom and Dad have been planning this morning for a month. They have selected gifts for each child, unique to their liking. Christmas breakfast is a curated collection of each child's favorite foods and beverages. Mom and Dad took great care in wrapping each gift and making it something exciting to see, even on the outside. As the kids wake up and bound through the living room to the Christmas tree, Mom and Dad are just as excited as the kids for what is to be revealed. They know the contents of each gift, but the opportunity to surprise and delight each child fills them with anticipatory pride. The parents' joy has already been extended, but they buzz to see the expressions of wonder and glee as each gift is revealed. As packages are presented, squeals and cheers ensue. The experience of Christmas morning is a great example of how our gifts and talents are placed inside of us for us to discover. Just as good parents know what their children like and desire to give them good gifts, God has placed gifts inside of each of us that He knows will bring contentment and satisfaction. However, to experience the benefits, we have to open the packages and discover what is inside of each one. In the case of Christmas gifts, these same items would be enjoyable to the children if they had been at the store to pick them out with their parents. However, the *process* of discovery increased the delight and satisfaction in each gift because it offered participatory joy through the process of discovery.

Each individual has a unique set of characteristics and experiences that inform their purpose. Just as it would be lackluster to open gifts that were all the same, the uniqueness of our purpose is critical. However, uniqueness without meaning and connection could just as easily facilitate loneliness rather than a strong sense of purpose. If our individual purposes were so distinct that they drove self-consciousness or comparison, it could lead to hiding or puffing up our sense of self-importance. Rather, if we understand that the joy we feel when we experience our purpose is the rush or participation in God's plan, this discovery will lead us to worship and service. Our purpose should drive us toward relationships with people. Said another way, our purpose should be embodied, connected.

The digital era in which we find ourselves is an interesting social experiment. People can have their name and image go viral, generating mass influence and come to find this experience to be empty and meaningless. Social psychology researcher Jonathan Haidt outlines the impact that digital relationships and social media have had on the youngest generations among us. His contrast between face-to-face versus digital relationships primarily centers on the shallow root system and the disembodied nature of screen-mediated connection. He notes that relationships where there is a low barrier to entry (online relationships) versus relationships that have a high bar for entry (in-person, communal social relationships), motivating a relational investment, have created a threat to the overall quality of life and relationships for the youngest members of society. While I would not claim that a person cannot live out their purpose in an online environment, as that is certainly a domain for influence, I would note that we must consider ways that online-only influence might undercut the ability for individuals to fully experience the embodied connection with others that our purpose offers to us. As Haidt notes, the digital age, and social media specifically, promotes a level of social comparison and pressure that we have not historically experienced. This social comparison may lead individuals to mimic the gifts and abilities of others rather than fully explore the life that is uniquely theirs to live.

Purpose is fully realized in connection with others, but it is most cheapened when we live in a comparison hole. Each of us, individually, is an expression of God's collective plan for making all things new. He has prepared these works for us in advance. I cannot do your job, and you cannot do mine. In this way, while distinct for each of us, God designed purpose as connective tissue between us. Perhaps it connects us to ourselves and to God by providing a rich sense that our life has significance, and it knits us together as a community, which can prevent loneliness. The sooner we realize that we have gifts to offer people, the quicker we reap the benefits. Embarking on the journey of discovery is the first step to realizing our gifts and purpose.

## Stay the Course Despite Distractions

With so many distractions, it is easy to lose sight of the purpose buried in our everyday lives. William Wilberforce, a British politician, philanthropist, and key figure in the movement to abolish slavery in the 19th century, encouraged us to have our eyes open to the mundane when looking for what our unique purpose is. "We have different forms assigned to us in the school of life—different gifts imparted. All is not attractive that is good. Iron is useful, though it does not sparkle like the diamond. Gold has not the fragrance of a flower. So different persons have various modes of excellence, and we must have an eye to all." We must keep an eye on what our purpose looks like. Maybe we are looking at the world in front of us through the lens of comparison, wishing for a different set of talents. Sometimes, life's disappointments cloud our vision. Often, it takes a little digging to uncover purpose. While God's plan is clear to Him, we don't always have that same clarity. We may not yet understand how He intends to use the features of our design or make meaning of our heartaches. In fact, sometimes we misunderstand His intention. We need a way to uncover the elements that create our unique purpose formula and how we impact the world.

## Our Purpose May Be Ordinary

Sometimes, the ability to articulate and appreciate our purpose only becomes apparent in retrospect. Meaning, we may be living our significant contribution and not be aware of it at the time. I imagine this to be true of the mothers of Mother Theresa, Billy Graham, or Albert Einstein. Did they realize what they were offering the world? How would their lives be commingled with history? Their contribution may not have been a humanitarian sacrifice, an evangelistic sermon, or a scientific theory; rather, it was someone they nurtured and took care of. Their purpose looked a lot like daily life. Sometimes, this conversation gets confused by the idea that our purpose has to have some kind of massive scale, supposing that rather than being small, it has to be grand to be important. Sometimes, purpose looks like faithfulness in the things that we have been given to steward. Sometimes, purpose looks ordinary, a sort of "as you are going" kind of contribution. In this way, we can take comfort in our mundane purpose or steady life.

## Joseph of Arimathea

When I think about someone who may have best understood his purpose by looking at the past, I think of Joseph of Arimathea.

We know very little about Joseph of Arimathea. His story is only a few lines in the Bible. We know from Scripture that he was wealthy, although we don't know how he made his money. We also know that he was a spiritual man, described in Mark 15:43 as a "prominent member of the [Jewish] council...waiting for the kingdom of God." In Matthew 27:57, we learn that he was a secret disciple of Jesus, which would have been controversial given the hysteria of the time around this prophet. We can assume that he was brave and an independent thinker because he did not go along with the council's recommendation to crucify Jesus. The gospel writer Mark notes that Joseph "boldly approached Pilate" to ask for the body of Jesus while he was still hanging on the cross. This was the first that Pilate knew of Jesus' final death, and Scripture states that Pilate was "surprised" (Mark 15:44) that Jesus was already dead. Joseph's zeal for Jesus was impatient and assuming. We know from extra biblical texts that Joseph was later confronted by the council.

In the Gospel of Nicodemus, the Jewish elders express anger at Joseph for burying the body of Christ, saying:

> "Why are you angry against me because I begged the body of Jesus? Behold, I have put him in my new tomb, wrapping in clean linen and I have rolled a stone to the door of the tomb. And you have acted not well against the just man, because you have not repented of crucifying him, but also have pierced him with a spear."
>
> *Gospel of Nicodemus.*

Assuming that Joseph was speaking for himself, we observe his rational and resolute mindset toward what he had done. Joseph assumed responsibility for burying Jesus, seemingly with no pressure from other Jesus followers or input from the disciples, rather, facing great personal pressure from his peers.

This act was a fulfillment of prophetic scripture (Isaiah 53:9) where it says the Messiah was *laid with the rich* in his burial. This pronouncement was made hundreds of years before the time of Christ. Burying Christ was a good work that God had initiated well ahead of time for Joseph to complete. It is unlikely that Joseph considered himself to be a fulfillment of this prophecy. Rather, he was doing the good thing in front of him out of faithfulness. We know that Joseph buried Jesus in his own tomb, using his own resources to purchase linen to wrap his body. He secured the tomb with a large stone where the Roman guards were eventually stationed.

Joseph was prominent among the wealthy Jewish influencers of his day. Yet, if he had not chosen to be faithful, even confrontational, he would have been an otherwise unknown and unremarkable rich guy. While it cannot be said that Joseph changed the world, God arranged for his story to be a part of the greatest story in history by the use of his bold personality and wealth to realize a significant contribution. Faithful in the ordinary, he lived his purpose.

We can take several lessons from the life of Joseph of Arimathea as we embark on our own journey to discovering our purpose. We see that just as Scripture says, God is a rewarder of those who earnestly seek him (Hebrews 11:6). Joseph's contribution unfolded from his purpose. If we seek to understand the unique ways that God designed for us to impact the world, as He fulfilled in Joseph of Arimathea, God will reward our request to live in our purpose.

Joseph's bold, independent, and strong personality are likely the very characteristics that made him successful and wealthy.

God intentionally gave you your personality characteristics, talents, and abilities; it's not a coincidence. They are resources to aid your sense of purpose and likely clues to discovering what God has planned for your life. If you have ever felt like you were "too much" or "not enough" to make an impact, God has a different perspective and desires for you to see His reasoning for these unique design features.

Finally, we also see that we don't always need to know our impact to live our purpose. It is unlikely that Joseph of Arimathea recognized how his personal generosity and choices would impact the story of the Messiah. He acted in faith, but we don't know if he thought the tomb was a temporary or permanent gift to Jesus. He did a good deed, and thousands of years later, we see his life as a meaningful reference for our lives. Only God has the power to create that kind of echo across eternity. We cannot manufacture impact. While we can pursue our purpose and seek to live it out faithfully, the magnitude of impact can only be measured by the One who created and set everything in motion.

## What I Didn't Expect

There is great irony in the confidence of youth. We know the least when we are young, yet we feel the most exuberance to try. It is nearly cruel that as we age and are seasoned by knowledge, experiences, and disappointments, our zeal to pursue new things changes. We move through life, gain more knowledge, and are simultaneously paralyzed by it. There is much discussion on the role of trauma in our world today. If you watch social media, trauma trends and categorizes itself through silly hashtags and comments that align toward shared experience. The common refrain is "We all have trauma, you just haven't found yours yet." Once you do, you can attach your personal pronoun, "me/my trauma," and join the club. It occurs to me this may be one of the sneakiest purpose-stealing tricks that exists today. I don't want to minimize the impact that trauma can have on an individual; I just want to highlight how our everyday, ordinary, and acute extraordinary human experiences are the very places where we can be surprised by God, who purposefully heals us.

There are some things that a person can understand on an intellectual level that can only become personal understanding through lived experience. This is the role that I think our ordinary days play in helping us discover our own sense of purpose. These are the opportunities that our most gut-wrenching and mundane experiences offer. Wounds become healed scars when we work through our pain with the one who can reset our narrative from trauma to wisdom. Living our stories with purpose and meaning is the intended outcome for all of us. Submitting to pain and boredom in our daily lives deepens our knowledge of ourselves and God.

It is not always obvious the way that God is walking with me. Sometimes, the clearest way to see God's hand has been in the rearview. However, the longer I seek His heart toward me, the more the eyes of my heart are opened to view the ordinary as an opportunity to deepen in wisdom and love toward God and others rather than as an option to despair.

## What Is Your Chief End?

The first question in the Westminster Shorter catechism asks, "What is the chief end of man?" The answer is, "Man's chief end is to glorify God and enjoy him forever." For the Christian, the goal or purpose of our lives is to glorify and enjoy God. Expressing our unique purpose is one avenue through which we simultaneously glorify and enjoy Him as an intertwined experience. As we seek to locate and live out the purpose of our lives, we get to encounter God as we move in the direction of His intended impact for our lives. He is with us, moving through us. As it states in Acts 17:28, "In him, we live and move and have our being." When we are awake to our purpose, it brings meaning and life to even the most mundane tasks of life.

Do you know *and* live? We know there are at least three primary experiences for people: those who know their purpose and are living it, those who are unsure of their purpose and need to discover it, and those who are discouraged in their purpose and feel stuck. Whichever place you find yourself, the following chapters will support your journey toward clarity.

I hope to fan the flames for those of you who are running hard after your purpose. It's time to describe and define your unique purpose formula. For those who are discouraged, I hope you find the energy to get up and go again today. And for the third group, I hope that you experience the spark of what it is to live and lead with purpose. There is truly no other way to live.

# CHAPTER 2

# WHAT IS PURPOSE?

"Many persons have a wrong idea of what constitutes true happiness. It is not attained through self-gratification but through fidelity to a worthy purpose."
—Helen Keller

In the 1989 blockbuster hit *The Little Mermaid*, Ariel, born mermaid royalty, falls in love with Prince Eric, who happens to be a human. She had always been obsessed with ship-wrecked treasures that she found at the bottom of the sea. Ariel dreams of having legs and walking on land. Her wish comes true through an evil trade with the notorious sea witch, Ursula.

While sitting at dinner in the castle, Ariel sees one of her sea treasures, the "dinglehopper," next to her place setting. Quickly picking up the dinglehopper, she begins to run the human fork through her hair. It is humorous because she is using an object that is designed for an entirely different purpose outside of its intended use.

In a similar way, we often pick up skills, jobs, and talents and utilize them outside of our intended design. We can do work that is unsuited to our talents. We may actually be good at the work but struggle to find joy in it. We can play roles that are designed for others merely because we haven't realized that we have strengths, desires, and insights that are meant to be deployed specifically. If we find that purpose, life takes on a deeper meaning, our soul begins to fully flourish.

I love watching this movie with my own daughters to see if they pick up the humor, instruction, and warning that the film offers us. As a parent, I view King Triton differently as a loving rather than restrictive father. He wants what is best for Ariel and knows that there are ways that she is designed that are features rather than flaws. Like Ariel, we can often wish we were more like someone else, "a part of their world." Where our story and Ariel's diverge is that we were created exactly as we were meant to be with the requisite personality, potential, and option to develop that will help us flourish in the world. While we actually need to develop and mature our potential, we do not need to become someone besides who we are in order to live the life we were meant to live.

## Flourish

Flourishing is a term that is well studied in psychology and is used to describe a person who experiences fulfillment and meaning in their life. Human flourishing is defined as an effort to achieve self-actualization and fulfillment within the context of a larger community of individuals, each with the right to pursue his or her own such efforts. The idea of human flourishing as critical to a life well-lived is an ancient one. In fact, Socrates (c. 470–399 BCE) believed that the purpose of life was to achieve eudaimonia, often translated as "flourishing" or "the good life." He argued that this could be accomplished through virtuous living, a commitment to self-examination, and the pursuit of wisdom. Socrates saw purpose as rooted in understanding oneself and living a life aligned with truth, even if it challenged social norms. For him, knowledge was inherently linked to virtue, and virtue was essential to fulfilling one's true purpose. Similarly, Confucius (551–479 BCE) held influential ideas on purpose in ancient philosophy. He believed the purpose of life was to cultivate virtue (*ren*) and fulfill one's roles and duties, especially within relationships and society. Confucius emphasized harmonious social relationships, ethical behavior, and moral self-cultivation. According to him, fulfilling one's purpose meant living virtuously, respecting tradition, and seeking to improve oneself and one's community.

According to these ideas, human flourishing is both a personal and collective good. In other words, my life is inextricably linked to yours. It stands to reason that when people feel like their life is connected and meaningful, it benefits society as a whole. When individuals are optimistic, hopeful, and others-focused, social fabrics cannot help but be strengthened. One paralleling idea from the field of organizational psychology is that workforce engagement and productivity are improved when organizational and individual purposes are aligned. Larger communal improvement, in this case, an organization, is an output of individuals who are able to achieve personally meaningful goals. If we are to define purpose as only being true purpose in so much as it connects to a larger sense of service to humanity, one would naturally expect there to be a symbiotic relationship between the part and the whole.

According to modern psychologists, purpose is a key component of human flourishing. "Purpose in life represents a stable and generalized intention to accomplish something that is at once personally meaningful and at the same time leads to productive engagement with some aspect of the world beyond the self. " Notably, according to this definition, purpose represents at least three components: long-term orientation, personal significance, and others' orientation. There it is again, the inter-connection of personal and collective good. This benefit seems to elude many. According to a research study recently published by Lifeway, the majority of Americans (57%) regularly wonder about how to find more purpose in their lives. This means if people are not personally waking up asking this question, then they are regularly feeling some level of dread as they get ready for the day. Without a strong sense of purpose, answering questions of personal motivation and drive is difficult. Given the personal and communal components of purpose, daily dread has a compounding impact on overall personal and societal wellness. "Lack of direction/purpose could contribute to anxiety/depression; experiencing depression/anxiety could contribute to less motivation and participation in things that used to give purpose; or they could compound each other." Withdrawal from one's purpose means that the likely recipient of that contribution will not benefit from the opportunity their contribution offers.

Research indicates that a robust sense of purpose is a hallmark of someone who is mentally well. The contrasted concept is someone who lacks purpose and finds themselves languishing or eventually becomes depressed. Therapy can help us process our unhappiness and discontent. One of the chief aims of therapy is to encourage individuals to find their unique ability to flourish by making positive forward movement toward meaningful goals. The rise in popularity in discussing and seeking therapy is an indicator that we are not well as a society. Many therapists are reporting a sharp increase in the number of individuals seeking support for anxiety and depression.

## How Purpose Helped Me Flourish

With the word flourish, the image of a garden and seeds comes to mind. As my good friend and author Jeremie Kubicek says, people are a lot like plants. Plants need sunlight and water to grow. Similarly, people need support and challenge. In order for our purpose to be empowered, we need to set the conditions that support the opportunity to grow. The truth about purpose, however, is that we are not always in seasons of blooming. We may be in a watering season, pruning season, or even letting the ground lay fallow as a means of recovering from a season of high production. Dominating ourselves for lack of productive fruit is a malforming behavior when it comes to flourishing in our sense of purpose.

One of my favorite questions to ask myself and clients in my consulting practice is, "What does healthy look like?" When we understand seasons of purpose through an agrarian lens, it can help us properly tend the garden or purpose in our lives. When I lose sight of the many phases of living in my purpose, it can be easy to panic or put pressure on myself to produce when it is not the season to do that. In winter, a healthy plant does not produce fruit. If we were to judge that plant on its fruit production during winter only, it may be deemed as a useless plant. However, when we properly view the plant, tending it in season and out, providing it what it needs to grow…grow it does. Plants are designed to grow. So are we.

Rather than grow into our potential and purpose, however, many turn to coping mechanisms and even addiction. We are dealing with a failure to flourish in acceptable and unacceptable ways. Many are turning to tech-mediated solutions to find connection and meaning.

## Online & Disconnected

In a post-pandemic, fully digitized world, we are as disconnected and lonely as we have ever been. In fact, one study explored the connection between digitization and mental health. Their methodology displayed that there has been a sharp increase in depression and anxiety correlated to the amount of time spent online.

According to the World Health Organization, the pandemic triggered a 25% increase in anxiety and depression worldwide. That increase presented itself against an already bleak global reality. Prior to 2020, depression and anxiety were leading causes of global health-related burdens. The growing body of research indicates that the more purposeful or meaningful a person's life, the higher quality and longer their life will be. With the expansion of technology, digitization, and AI solutions, we may be improving knowledge access and extending lifespan, but how are we impacting human flourishing? How are tech leaders accounting for the pursuit of purpose? Lengthening life and eliminating disease reduces suffering. However, these solutions will lack joy if we do not know how to identify our purpose, which translates to a deepened sense of well-being.

Technology has impacted our wellness in negative and positive ways. Particularly, social media has introduced pervasive comparison, surface connection, and image curation, to name a few of the challenges. The potential negative influence of these phenomena might be curbed through the pursuit of substance over surface. As individuals seek to truly answer the question of meaning and learn to pursue purpose, they may find that the answer to this modern existential crisis is actually an ancient one.

The silver lining in the digital age may appear as a craving for more. As individuals begin to understand endless opportunities, they engage in the digital world, which leads to impactful action. The pursuit of flourishing may be a contemporary reference, but its original intent goes back several thousand years to the time of Jesus. He declared the mission of His own life to be the embodiment of a purposeful human existence. Jesus declared that the reason He came was so that we could have a full life (John 10:10). His mission extends to modern America. Put simply, Jesus lived so that we could access an abundant life. If we live out that declaration, we must pursue true human flourishing through the full expression of our life, lived with purpose. As it usually turns out, science documents what Jesus declared to be true. When we find our purpose and live it, we bring a unique expression of His strategic plan for the planet to bear. Discovering our purpose and living it out is a redemptive expression.

Self-awareness and self-differentiation lead to greater engagement with the world. It makes us different from others so that we can make unique and meaningful contributions to the world. Knowing your purpose strengthens your sense of self; it gives you a way to explain who you are both to other people and yourself.

According to Victor Frankl, Austrian psychiatrist, Holocaust survivor, and father of much of the seminal literature on purpose, having a "concrete assignment that demands fulfillment" allows us to see ourselves as essential. We recognize that we cannot be replaced by anyone else. This sense of being needed connects us to others in a way that reminds us to continue on when times get tough. When we know someone is counting on us to show up, it changes the way we show up. When I get invited to a party or event, I need a job to do. It makes me feel more comfortable at the event, and it also requires my attendance. If I know people are counting on me to bring something or to complete a role, I have to come and cannot give into my introverted regret of saying, "Yes, I will attend." I co-lead a group in the city where I live that is a fairly large networking event. Six years ago, you could not have paid me money to attend a networking event, and now I lead one. I emcee the event to ensure that we stay on schedule, people feel welcome, and that the program flows well. If I don't attend, I have to make sure someone is prepared to do my job. It makes me think twice about scheduling over the event, and since I have a unique role to play, that event takes priority in my calendar. I have an assignment that demands fulfillment.

People want to feel like they matter. It is not silly to want to have your absence noticed or your presence needed. This may be why so many young people long to be unique, different, or famous. The craving that often expresses itself as eccentricity may actually be the desire to be significant and irreplaceable. It is a desire to be needed. The need to be needed feels nearly primal, calling forth our development into someone who matters to others in a unique and meaningful way. Our responsibility to lead a life of purpose that positively impacts others is not a calling to narcissistic grandeur; rather it is a human need to mean something to others. To be purposefully connected.

## Specific, Not Generic

One of the common misconceptions about purpose is that human purpose is generic. In fact, Christians can make these mistakes most frequently by assuming that the Great Commission is a blanket statement to be pursued without nuance or regard for the way in which God has set us toward a unique purpose. I think this sweeping mistake contributes to languishing or lazy acceptance that our life is insignificant. We are inadvertently creating a bystander effect with regard to purpose. You have been given a unique, significant purpose that cannot be fulfilled by anyone else, but you must pursue that truth with confidence.

Patrick Hill, a research psychologist from the University of Washington, developed a framework for understanding purpose called the PATHS model (Purpose as Trait, Habit, and State). The PATHS model defines purpose as a developmental journey that is both directional, habitual, and situational based on the activities that we engage in. This framework is congruent with the patterns we see in Scripture. Our individual purposes are moving in the direction of eternity with overarching meaning (that is, the trait), and they are reinforced by the habits we allow and the situations in which we engage (we reap what we sow). Hill would refer to this as living a purposeful life.

In Ecclesiastes, chapter three, we see that God made us long for something beyond ourselves. It is a human trait to long for something more. Yet we also know that the life we live impacts the experience we have on earth. We reap what we sow. What we do habitually determines whether or not our life is filled with or void of purpose. Our life decisions reinforce or undermine our purpose. Our temporal experience is meant to be meaningful in that it leads us to a greater connection with others and, ultimately, with God. To borrow from Hill, purpose is a path to be pursued because it is both innate and influenceable.

One could perceive connection to larger humanity as having the potential to generate homogeneity. Connectedness, however, does not mean uniformity. In fact, the uniqueness of your life has an intended impact for this time in history. This truth should free us from the pressure to compare our contribution or pursuit of purpose to other people. God designed each human with a desire to activate their purpose. It is a gift that we can explore this design and experience the joy in discovery. When we tap into that significance, everything shifts because we experience the congruence that comes from living according to our masterful design.

God wants us to experience the energetic gift of flourishing that living with purpose brings. It is a fire He longs to ignite inside of us. God created us to make a difference. However, He is not obligated to ensure that we activate our potential. Living a life of purpose is a partnership between His design and our actions. We have to intentionally pursue our purpose to participate in the meaning that purpose brings. We miss out when we don't pursue our purpose. Moreover, others also miss out on our gift when we don't live our purpose. The purpose of God will prevail, but our experience will be compromised. Discovering our purpose is a critical element of being fully alive.

Here's an anecdote: if you have a gas stove or fireplace in your home like I do, you know that the fireplace possesses the potential to heat the room. You probably are familiar with what it is to light the flame. It takes several sparks to finally see the blue flame. When the pilot light is burning, it effectively uses the fuel toward its intended purpose, bringing warmth to the room.

Similarly, to activate our own potential life of purpose, it may require several sparks to light the pilot light of our souls. Our souls, when sparked with purpose, bring warmth, meaning, and unique energy to the work that we do. Purpose-driven work is a game-changer for how we serve others. Purpose answers the long-standing question, "Why am I here?" It gives meaning to our lives, preventing hopelessness—pulling us toward a future of hope.

It is easy to float along and not pursue the discovery of our unique purpose. Purpose must be pursued and unpacked. There are three elements that spark our understanding of our unique purpose. Those three elements are our design, our desires, and our disappointments. Through reflecting on and understanding ourselves and the unique features that make up who we are, we can discover the purpose that reveals our unique contribution.

Reflection plays a crucial role in discovering our purpose as it allows us to take a step back and truly understand ourselves, our values, and our goals. By taking the time to reflect on our experiences, successes, failures, and desires, we are able to gain clarity and perspective on what truly matters to us. Furthermore, reflection helps us to identify patterns in our thoughts, emotions, and behaviors that may point toward our true passions and interests. Through introspection and self-examination, we can uncover our strengths, weaknesses, and areas for growth, which can ultimately guide us toward our purpose.

Regular reflection helps us reassess our goals and priorities, ensuring that we align our actions with our values and move towards a fulfilling and meaningful life. By taking the time to reflect on our past choices and experiences, we can make informed decisions about our future path and make necessary adjustments to stay true to ourselves. In essence, reflection is essential in discovering our purpose as it prompts us to delve deep into our inner selves, gain clarity on our values and goals, and make intentional choices that lead us toward a life filled with passion, fulfillment, and purpose.

## Box of Matches

"My candle burns at both ends;

It will not last the night;

But ah, my foes, and oh, my friends—

It gives a lovely light!"

Edna St. Vincent Millay

The following chapters will give you opportunities to reflect on your past experiences and help you explore your story so you can find your purpose, add fuel to an already burning fire, or find energy to once again light the flame of your purpose. You were designed on purpose, for a purpose, and born into this time in history to pour it out for others. Let's explore that together and find your unique purpose formula.

You and I don't get to choose how long we are here, but we do get to choose if we will strike the match. There are many un-lit candles. The passion I have for you to be lit up by purpose is from experiencing it myself. No one wants to look back on their life and wonder, "What if?"

# CHAPTER 3
# FINDING PURPOSE?

"Adventure is worthwhile in itself."
—Amelia Earhart

One of my favorite moments was realizing I was right in the middle of an adventure. Maybe you've had the moment of pinching yourself and saying to yourself, "Don't miss this." For me, the feeling was one of a train pulling away from the station. I had the option to get on the train or not, but I knew the choice to stay on the platform was going to mean that I was missing something great.

In January of 2018, I had several very significant people in my life ask me the same question, "Jessica, what do you want?" I was stunned by such a simple question or rather my lack of ability to answer it. I was nearly finished with my doctoral degree, and it felt like a mountain just inches from my face. I could not see past the fog and the face of the base. What I wanted was a question I could not seem to find the answer to when such a mass was in front of me. I pondered and pondered, letting my mind seek a good answer. But the truth was I did not know and honestly was too numb from the weight of responsibilities and stress to identify any desires at all.

I remembered a prayer that David prayed in Psalm 38:9 (BSB), "O Lord, my every desire is before You; my groaning is not hidden from you." I prayed, *God, I don't know what I want, but I know You do. Will You show me?* Over the next several months, God began to highlight things for me that made it clear what I wanted. I had a sense of dissatisfaction that I had ignored. I was good at what I was doing and honestly loved the impact that I was making, yet the nagging unanswered question of desire persisted. Eventually, God made it clear to me that He was leading me toward a major career change. I argued, "But God, I'm not done with this degree yet. I'm studying this program so I can be better at my current role. I love this job."

If you had asked me before I opened myself up to answering that question of what I wanted, I would have told you that I was working in a way that was well aligned to my purpose... and that would have been true. However, God was inviting me on a new adventure. God is very interested in our hearts becoming fully alive to the chances He is offering us. Discovering what those ventures are is part of the wonder.

Given the role that purpose plays in wellness and a full life, why would it not be more apparent to us what we are meant to do? For some, finding purpose feels like a divine scavenger hunt. God could have made it more obvious. It could be deemed cruel that finding one's purpose boils down to a hunt, especially if you are the type of person who likes to flip to the last page of a book to see the ending. "The thrill of the chase" represents the idea that there is joy to be found in the pursuit of something. We also know that when there is an element of difficulty in such a pursuit, that hard element actually sweetens the task. Thanks to the work of neuroscience, we may be starting to understand the mechanisms that lie behind this popular phrase. According to research, the more that we push ourselves toward goal achievement, particularly when there is a challenge involved, the more our brain chemicals reward our overall system. As we focus and pursue a skill or ability that requires development and learning, the more satisfaction we experience as we gain mastery of those skills. According to neuroscience enthusiast Dr. Andrew Huberman, dopamine levels control our desire. "Dopamine is responsible for motivation and drive, primarily at the psychological level, also for craving." As we pursue things from which we derive joy, we train our brains to crave that continued resource. "So if I were to just put a really simple message around dopamine, it would be: 'There's a molecule in your brain and body that when released tends to make you look outside yourself, pursue things outside yourself, and to crave things outside yourself." What this means is it may be that even our biological systems are set up to support the pursuit of purpose and meaning. The *thrill* of the chase, therefore, is scientifically evident. Our system rewards us as we pursue meaning.

Perhaps the beauty found in the chase is exactly what God had in mind when He created each of us. God is offering us a pathway to deep contentment and satisfaction, but finding purpose requires pursuit. We must explore unique aspects of ourselves. He has planted clues into our design that are like Easter eggs. Once we find them, we can activate our unique formula. It isn't just the pursuit of purpose that brings about reward. Purpose is a fundamental contribution that we make toward the greater good. Our unique purpose, when activated, won't be an insular or self-focused experience. It will be an expression of God's love for the planet, expressed through each person toward others. Purpose will drive us to service. With this impact in mind, it is important that we bring awareness to each element so that we can be intentional with our actions. Pursuing purpose is a choice we make to be others-oriented and make an impact on the world around us. Purpose is a lifelong pursuit.

Purpose didn't just give me a sense of meaning. It made me move. I believe you and I are made for the greater chase. The breath of God is in our moving and being. He has orchestrated our movement toward a meaningful contribution. It was common ancient Greek operating philosophy that the gods, Zeus particularly, "awakens us to work, reminding us of our livelihood." In other words, we are to get up and move, pursue something daily that binds us to common humanity. Connecting to this idea, in Acts 17:28, Luke writes, "in Him we live and move and have our being." This idea of movement and pursuit is critical for us to grasp. All of these concepts elicit a sense of being fully alive. What are you pursuing? What makes you move?

Oftentimes, the clues that point to purpose feel like sparks in our soul, similar to those sparks that light a pilot light. Educators often seek moments of learning or "lightbulb moment" when a spark of insight or a dim concept suddenly becomes clear or illuminated to the students. These sparks are energetic in nature. When we are children, these insights are fluid and happen in the form of play and interests. Anyone who interacts with children observes how interests and curiosity drive learning. I have a nephew who is fascinated by holes in the ground. We can't pass a storm drain in the neighborhood without stopping to explore. He sticks his face against the grates, peering to the bottom of a dark abyss. Prior to his spark of interest, I had walked past these same drains hundreds of times. It had never caught my interest. Something very common and almost dismissable to me was of major importance to him. It will be interesting to see how this fascination might play into his future purpose.

Peter Benson related these "sparks" of interest to purpose and noted how often our adult purposes can be traced back to our interests in childhood. Studies find that creative arts, athletics, and learning are the most commonly reported sparks; others include volunteering, reading, spending time in nature, and engaging in spiritual practices. Interestingly, he also noted that there is a critical role that adults can play for children as they begin to experience the sparks of interest that might unfold into future purpose. He goes on to say, "Children who can identify their spark and who can point to adults who recognize it show enhanced signs of physical and psychological well-being, excel in school, and are more likely to strive to contribute to the world beyond themselves, which is an important element of purpose. In this way, nurturing children's sparks can set the stage for purpose. We are to fan flames that spark creativity and interest.

Often, these sparks are a path of curiosity. Dr. Andrew Huberman defines curiosity as a "strong interest in knowing something but without an attachment to the outcome." Initially, curiosity sparks something inside of us, like my nephew and the holes. We just have to know. What do we have to know? The outcome is likely unknown but there is just something inherently interesting in the pursuit of the object of our curiosity. Curiosity and surprise are closely linked. Dr. Lex Friedman, a computer science and AI researcher, refers to the intersection of curiosity and surprise as "magic." Moments of surprise are likely the reward a curious mind seeks. We are looking for moments of magic on earth.

Curiosity is a mechanism for finding the happiness that surprises can offer. Curiosity, however, is uniquely personal. "*Curiosity is a fundamental human trait. Everyone is curious, but the object and degree of that curiosity is different depending on the person and the situa-*

*tion.*" There are so many stories of individuals who have made scientific breakthroughs. Yet, to the scientist, the breakthrough moment was only part of the reward. An insatiable, curious desire to pursue insight was a reward. According to Britannica Curiosity Compass, there is a distinct difference between knowledge-seeking and curiosity. That difference comes down to the locus of our motivation, internal or external. If we are driven to find answers due to external needs (i.e., our teacher assigned homework, and it is graded), that activity is considered knowledge seeking.

However, if we are pursuing knowledge because of internal needs (i.e., I take apart an engine just to see how it works), we are engaged in a curious behavior. Curiosity is, by definition, an internal pursuit of knowledge. It is an appetite that is uniquely yours. Epistemic curiosity is the desire to close specific knowledge gaps (when we research a topic to understand), and empathetic curiosity is our desire to better understand relationships and people. We may have a stronger preference for one or the other based on our wiring and comfort level. Epistemic and empathetic curiosity help us identify our unique bends toward particular areas of interest.

Maybe you are reading this as an adult and have no clue what your purpose is. You don't have a way to articulate your unique contribution. The good news is that it is never too late to get curious. It is not too late to look backward for clues and put together patterns based on past and present knowledge of yourself. We can also engage community and relationships to flame the pattern of our purpose. We may even notice that God has been working things together for good over time, even though we have been unaware.

The purpose formula is P=(D+D+D)*V. Purpose equals design plus desires plus disappointments multiplied by God's vision for impact. We'll explore each element of the formula and apply it uniquely to you. The role of the purpose formula is not to say that your purpose must be discovered through this formula. You can explore each element of the formula and increase your own self-awareness and, thereby, your ability to live with intentionality in the world around you.

In each of the following chapters, I will unpack each element of the purpose formula. At the end of each chapter, there will be reflective questions to digest your unique experiences and wiring. At the end of the book, I will endeavor to help you put it all together. However, if you are anything like me, you may need to walk away from the book and digest a little bit. There may be a need to dialogue with people who love you to ensure that you are being honest but not overly harsh. You may need to process some of your deeper disappointments before you can recognize your purpose. It is not always easy to articulate the ways in which you are poised to impact those around you. However, I'm happy that you are on this journey with me and grateful that you are trusting these concepts as your guide.

It is my prayer that this journey encourages you. I hope that you will see the ways God has gifted you and set you in this time and place with meaningful intention. Your life matters. People in your world need you fully alive. Be fully alive. Purposefully alive.

# CHAPTER 4

# DESIGN

"For you created my inmost being; you knit me together in my mother's womb. I praise you because I am fearfully and wonderfully made; your works are wonderful, I know that full well. My frame was not hidden from you when I was made in the secret place, when I was woven together in the depths of the earth. Your eyes saw my unformed body; all the days ordained for me were written in your book before one of them came to be.."
—Psalm 139:13-16

When God went to work on us in our mother's womb, He knit purpose into our hearts. He planted longings and talents inside of us that would one day bear fruit in His timing. We see that He planned ahead for us, placing us in His greater purpose. The psalmist writes that all of our days are "ordained" for us. Ordained means that our life has been established with a measure of authority. He has designed us *with* a purpose and *for* a purpose for this time period. When I say we are designed with a purpose, I'm talking about the fact that God has a unique story for us to tell with our lives. Our life has inherent value. God is with us and intimately invested in each moment we breathe. Our story is woven into the greater narrative of humanity. We are part of a historical tale and have been grafted into a larger, meaningful drama of a metanarrative.

The psalmist states that all the days were written before they came to be. While we are connected to God's greater story, our days are unique to the plans He has for us, and our design is fitted to that purpose. This intentionality is why it is so important that we don't try to live out someone else's purpose. God has a complex master plan for the world. He is delighted to deploy our talents and skills according to his plan. He desires to set us on a purposeful path that connects to His larger kingdom plans. Ephesians 2:10 states, "For we are God's handiwork, created in Christ Jesus to do good works which God prepared in advance for us to do."

I studied art as an undergraduate student. In that pursuit, we had to study the works of the great artists of history. We studied their masterpieces. A masterpiece is the grand work of an artist. It is considered to be their crowning achievement. We know many of these by name, *The Mona Lisa* by da Vinci or *Starry Night* by van Gogh. Those well-known works had value because they were made by a great artist. It was their creator who bestowed value upon them merely because the piece was a product of their artistry. Similarly, as an outflow of the creative work of God, we are of the greatest value due to the value bestowed on us by God, the greatest artist of all. He designed us to be a display of His glory. The fruit we bear is a testament to His magnificence.

Our design has several facets. It is important that we have an awareness of our design features if we are to wield them to God's approval. We should not, however, feel pressure to figure it all out at once. We often have the best insights around our design as we live. God allows us to be exploratory in our pursuit of

His pathway. We have a unique design according to His diverse, complex plan.

## Personality

To quote the famous philosopher Socrates, one must "know thyself" in order to live a good life. The value of understanding ourselves is directional and preventative. If we understand our design, we can move in harmony with that design. Much like a vehicle operating with the proper fuel for its engine. "A lack of self-knowledge leaves you open to accidents and mistaken ambition. Armed with the right sort of self-knowledge, we have a greater chance of avoiding errors in our dealings with others and in the formulation of our life choices."

We are different from others on purpose. O.S. Guiness writes, "recognizing who we aren't is only the first step to knowing who we are." We must come to the realization that our unique differences are intentional design features. Whether you are introverted or extroverted, a creative thinker or a convergent thinker, whether spontaneous or more planned, your unique design is a meaningful reflection of who the Designer intended you to be. Your personality is not a design flaw. There is nothing "wrong" with you. Rather, each aspect of your wiring contributes to life with purpose.

Our personality plays a significant role in how we approach the pursuit and uncovering of our purpose. Our personality can heavily influence the path we choose to follow our purpose. There are lots of great tools (5 Voices, Strengthsfinders, MBTI, etc.) that help us understand our personality. These tools give us a framework for understanding our unique talents. While self-awareness includes interaction with others, knowing ourselves is our responsibility. Felicia Day states, "Knowing yourself is life's eternal homework." We must strive to understand ourselves so we can operate in our purpose. My friend and author Steve Cockram likes to quip, "You never graduate from the school of self-awareness." We must stay perpetually enrolled so that we are continuously growing.

In essence, our personality serves as a guiding force in shaping our beliefs, attitudes, and behaviors as we strive to understand ourselves and our place in the world. By harnessing our unique traits and utilizing them to their fullest potential, we can enhance our self-awareness, align our actions with our values, and ultimately fulfill our purpose.

Understanding our personality is the key to self-awareness. Awareness alone, however, can lead us to self-pity or even a preoccupation with ourselves. Nothing leads us further away from serving others well than self-obsession. As we discover our tendencies, this becomes data for our choices so that we can lead ourselves and others well.

Let me illustrate this way. If you are an introvert and you are on a work trip where there are lots of meetings from sun-up to sundown and then optional late-night meetings, this personality data can help you make healthy choices that allow you to show up with your best energy to those around you. An extroverted colleague invites you to hang out for the after party at the bar, but you are feeling drained and run-down. You know that the next day, you are up for a big presentation. If you didn't understand that you are an introvert with a need to recharge alone, you might convince yourself to power through and deal with the consequences of being tired the next day. A wiser, more aware you would advise that you take that personality data and make a healthier choice. If you understand that you are wired to need quiet recharge time and your extroverted colleague is getting energy from the late-night event, you can honor your wiring, communicate your need, and go back to your hotel room, avoiding low energy over the next several days.

What does this have to do with purpose? Sometimes, when we don't understand our own personality, it can be tempting to mimic someone else. Meaning, we feel the need to show up as other people do rather than honoring our own design and contributions. The tendency to mimic others and their personality style or habits can end up being a draining experience, which translates to a less-than-authentic version of yourself.

Personality does not determine what we do but rather how we approach what we do. Understanding our personality is key to getting a sense of how God wants us to approach our purpose. For example, if our introverted friends are constantly in noisy and overstimulated environments, they may miss the opportunity to reflect and analyze. The overstimulation may distract them from their purpose. Conversely, our extroverted friends may suffer in a quiet and understimulating environment. The minimal interaction could restrain them, which prevents the full expression of their purpose. Knowing ourselves allows us to shed the comparison trap and authentically live out the purpose God has for each of us.

Malformation, however, has occurred for all of us. Under the pressure of pretending to be someone else, we bend and sometimes break our natural wiring. This malformation can lead to burnout or languishing simply because we are not operating with our unique design features intact. We know from Romans 11:29 that God's gifts and his plans are irrevocable. Expressly, our choices do not ruin the purposes of God for our lives. The things we dislike about our personality are not powerful enough to prevent us from experiencing the good works that God has planned for us. I haven't always believed or felt that this was true. There was plenty about me that I considered to be design flaws rather than design features. I would look at others and wonder why I wasn't more pleasant or naturally nicer. Why did I have so many opinions and speak my mind so freely? Why did I have to be so bossy? Why couldn't I just go with the flow? While it is true that I had plenty of rough personality edges to smooth, the raw ingredients were leadership qualities that God had designed into me...not flaws to eradicate.

God has intentionally designed each of us, and what we perceive to be undesirable characteristics are actually features, not flaws. We are His masterpiece, not His mosaic. Rather than attaching a tone of disappointment with questions like, "Why did You make me like this?" I had to learn to ask, "Since You did this on purpose, what was Your plan in making me this way?" Knowing that He didn't mistakenly burden me with my personality allows me to embrace my strengths and not flaws. As I grow in self-awareness and self-leadership, I can do so from a place of confidence instead of insecurity. This perspective allows me to pursue purpose without the trap of comparison.

## Reflect:

- What are some of the things about your personality that you have struggled to understand?

_____

_____

_____

_____

- What are the ways that God has designed you that you haven't considered to be features?

_____

_____

_____

_____

- What are the things about you that are uniquely good about your personality?

_____

_____

_____

_____

- What would others say makes you, you?

_____

_____

_____

_____

**Prayer:**

God help me to see the original intent of Your design with my personality. Help me to identify malformation and open up to Your healing hand. Speak to me about my true identity and who You see me to be.

Record anything that the Lord may be showing you about your personality:

_____

_____

_____

_____

## Talents

**"I feel God made me for a purpose, but he also made me**
**fast. And when I run–I feel his pleasure."**
**—Eric Liddell**

Talents are those things that we are good at naturally. Some of us are great singers or musicians. Others of us are instinctively curious and great at learning. There are individuals who are naturally gifted at bringing order to chaos. Still, others find it easy to create environments that make people feel welcome. While there are stage-worthy talents that others applaud, oftentimes, our talents are things that we can overlook because they seem normal and insignificant. Take, for instance, the friend who has a knack for spotting the exact right gift for any major or minor occasion. Or perhaps it is the friend who always knows the right thing to say. These things can be learned from books and cultivated, but often, our natural talents are those things that we might take for granted because they come to us so easily. Our talents are a critical aspect of the diverse plan that God has for the world. No matter the type of talent we have, God can use it. It would be easy to breeze over our talents as irrelevant to our purpose. However, we know that God wastes nothing. Os Guinness writes, "God normally calls us along the line of our giftedness, but the purpose of our giftedness is stewardship and service, not selfishness."

Developing our talents and testing their limits is an act of stewardship. Stewardship is defined as "the careful and responsible management of something entrusted to one's care." This idea is an appropriate framework for our talents because it carries with it the idea that our talents are something we hold for a time. God gives us our talents in their raw form, but it is up to us to develop those talents so that they can grow and mature. One of the most famous of Jesus' parables in the Gospels is often labeled the parable of the talents. In the scriptures, the talents are representative of money.

In this story, a man was planning to be away from his property for a long time. He called together a small group of stewards who would be responsible for the success of his property while he was away on business. The Bible said that the owner entrusted each man with a certain number of talents according to his own abilities (Matthew 25:15). This small detail helps us understand that each man was not equally capable. However, the owner took their abilities into account as he gave their assignments. After an extended period, he came back to settle accounts. The man who had been given the most talent duplicated his portion and returned twice as much back to the owner. For that effort, he was praised as faithful and trustworthy. The man who had been given the median amount grew his portion and was also credited as trustworthy. Finally, the man who had been given the smallest talent to steward came forward to settle his account. When the man explained that he was fearful of risking any of the money that the steward had entrusted to him and had therefore buried his talent, returning the potion in exactly the same amount he had been given, the owner had a harsh reply. Matthew 25:26 records, "But his master replied, 'You wicked, lazy servant .... you should have put my money on deposit with the bankers, so that when I returned I would have received it back with interest'" Then, the owner took from the one who had the least, giving his portion to the man who was faithful with the largest portion.

While the literal interpretation of the word translated as "talents" is talking about a numeration of money, it is interesting to me that the English language uses the word *talent*. If we take this parable symbolically, there is a natural parallel to how we should think about our own personal gifts and talents. God has given all of us different measures of abilities and talents. Some of us have major gifts and talents that look like a big deal. Others of us have smaller, more modest gifts. However, the size of the talent is not the opportunity. The opportunity is to take what we have given and to faithfully multiply its impact. Like the master in the parable, who was planning to return to see what the servants had done with what was given to them, God is looking at the talents He has given each of us. God wants to see what we will do with what we have. How will we grow and develop the talent to serve the purpose for which it was given? Will we look at the gifts of others through the lens of comparison and think, "*My talents are too small to develop.*" Will we be faithful and trustworthy, or will we be wicked and lazy? Whatever the size of our talents, we must recognize them and look for ways to faithfully steward those gifts.

When we focus on and leverage our talents, we are more likely to excel in certain areas and find fulfillment in our work. Furthermore, our talents can also help us make a unique contribution to the world. Os Guinness communicates, "In the biblical understanding of giftedness, gifts are never ours for ourselves. We have nothing that was not given us. Our gifts are ultimately

God's, we are only 'stewards'—responsible for the prudent management of property that is not our own. This is why our gifts are always 'ours for others,' whether in the community of Christ or the broader society outside, especially the neighbor in need." When we use our talents to serve others and make a positive impact, we enjoy a sense of purpose that goes beyond our own personal goals. By embracing and developing our talents, we can more fully realize our potential and fulfill our true calling in life.

Our talents can guide us toward activities and roles that align with our innate abilities and strengths. By recognizing and honing our talents, we can uncover our true passions and interests, leading us toward a sense of purpose and direction in our lives. Early in our lives, we recognize our talents by what we are praised or rewarded for. In a recent podcast interview, John Mark Comer, a leading thinker on spiritual formation, noted that early in life, our successes and affirmation around them give us a clue as to where to invest our energy. Early in life, praise and recognition play a role in helping us understand those things that have potential for impact on others.

Later in life, we should be more disconnected from the need for praise as a driver of action. Over the course of time, obsession with or desire for recognition can be a liability to living a purposeful life or extracting joy and learning from our talents. We should not rest on praise and success, thereby neglecting the development and mastery of our gifts; rather, we must continue to deepen our reliance on humility and action to help us see the ways in which God intends to multiply our gifts.

According to Richard Rohr, "During the second-half of life, success no longer teaches us anything. It still feels good, but we don't learn from it. Now we learn more from failure." This affirmation of the role of praise was helpful to me as I and others identify purpose. In Christian circles, an emphasis on humility can often imply that we should be blind to our talents and bend toward duty. Taking a note from Comer and Rohr, I would offer this nuance: Our talent, well developed, is a gift we offer back to God for the gift He has already given us. Talent recognition and affirmation, while containing the temptation for ego glorification, also help us invest our energy accordingly. What is our noble aim? Something good that is pursued without talent may be a hobby, but it will not be the center target of our purpose. Rather, our talent, defined and developed, is something to behold. A beautiful masterpiece presented to the Master.

When I was growing up, there was a song we used to sing in Sunday School. It went, "This little light of mine, I'm gonna let it shine. This little light of mine. I'm gonna let it shine. This little light of mine, I'm gonna let it shine. Let it shine. Let it Shine. Let it shine." The second verse asked, "Hide it under a bushel?" and the children would loudly shout, "No! I'm gonna let it shine." The idea behind the song is to let our light shine for Jesus. We must let the joy of Jesus shine with pride. Sometimes, our joy in Jesus is most illuminated in us when we are doing that for which we are most talented, recognizing that it is God Himself who equipped us with that very talent. Perhaps His goal in giving the gift was for us to let it shine.

One of the best stories of how talent and purpose intermingle is the story of Scottish sprinter and missionary Eric Liddell. His talent at running caught the attention of newspapers and competitors alike. He was best known for his 100-meter sprinting ability. However, the standout story that is recounted in the film *Chariots of Fire* recounts that Eric Liddell chose to compete in the 1924 Summer Olympics as a 400-meter runner. Anyone who has spent time on the track knows that the 400-meter run is a wildly different race than the 100-meter sprint. Liddell made this choice because of his dedication to taking Sundays off in an act of worship. The 100-meter heats were scheduled for Sunday, but the 400-meter heats were scheduled for a weekday, allowing him to honor both his talent and his faith. Liddell won the 400-meter race at the Paris Olympics and returned to his post as a missionary to the Chinese, where he lived the rest of his life. Famously, Liddell is quoted as saying, "I feel God made me for a purpose, but he also made me fast. And when I run–I feel his pleasure." He did not diminish his talent as merely a fleshly ability, and he did not dishonor his purpose of sharing Jesus as a missionary. Rather, we see that God elevated Liddell, using his talent as a method for allowing Liddell to share his faith boldly with the world and his teammates.

It's also important to note that he intentionally developed his talents. No athlete can compete at an Olympic level without intentional habits and training regimens that develop their talent into a high-level asset. As we age, there is a temptation to discard some of our early talents and relegate them to the "used to" pile. I'm not suggesting that any of us should injure ourselves in pursuit of Olympic gold; however, it may be that the talent we have could be used to serve our community. Perhaps we teach or coach someone, or maybe our talent is an indicator of something we should be doing as an entrepreneur rather than an employee. Talents come in many forms, and they should be explored.

Marian Williamson taps into why we might hide our talents under a bushel or hold back from fully developing them. Williamson writes in *A Return to Love*, "Our deepest fear is that we are powerful beyond measure. It is our light, not our darkness, that most frightens us. We ask ourselves, Who am I to be brilliant, gorgeous, talented, fabulous? Actually, who are you *not* to be? You are a child of God. Your playing small doesn't serve the world." It is a regular occurrence that we play small in our purpose. Maybe it is because of a false understanding of humility or a misunderstanding of our responsibility to develop our talents. True humility is understanding that God alone is the giver of the talents we have. Our outworking of those talents will look like neither an absorption of the glory nor a rejection of their use. Rather, true humility will be a grateful and participatory act of worship. Whatever motivates playing small, we must conquer that tendency if we are going to allow God's masterpiece to be on full display for His glory.

## Reflect:

- Are there any talents that you have discarded because they don't seem to be purposeful?

_____

_____

_____

_____

- Are you aware of your talents but playing small? Why do you think that is?

_____

_____

_____

_____

- Are there any ways in which you are innately gifted? How could this be a display of God's purposes for you?

_____

_____

_____

_____

- Ask 3-5 people who know you well what you are uniquely talented at.

_____

_____

_____

_____

## Prayer:

God, I know that You have made each of us unique. Help me see the things that You have put inside of me, which are unique talents and interests that are purposeful. Ignite in me the ability to hone those talents as a way of living out Your purpose for my life.

## Notes:

_____

_____

_____

_____

_____

_____

_____

_____

## Spiritual Giftedness

Our spiritual giftedness includes the God-given abilities that the Holy Spirit bestows on us at salvation and through the process of growing in our faith. In Ephesians, we see the five-fold ministry framework, where there were five distinct offices that Jesus created for the church so that believers can be prepared. "Christ himself gave the apostles, the prophets, the evangelists, the pastors and teachers to equip his people for acts of service so that the body of Christ may be built up" Ephesians 4:11-12. In this passage, we see the intermingling of our abilities and purpose. We must actively pursue our assignments with purpose.

In 1 Corinthians 12:1-7, we see that spiritual gifts have been distributed to all believers "for the common good." We see that some are given wisdom, knowledge, faith, healing, miracles, or prophecy. In every place we see the listing of gifts, we see that they are diverse and dispersed. Each person who is following Christ and has the Holy Spirit dwelling inside, has a gift or gifts that are given for the common good. These supernatural fortunes are meant to build up others. The benefit of awareness lies in the ability to activate the gift. Further, it allows for the participatory joy we discussed in the beginning of the book. Awareness of your gift is not crucial or necessary for the operation of the gift. There are many times when I will realize that my spiritual gifts have been in operation only by reflecting on the experience. However, as I have learned to notice the patterns of God using me beyond my natural abilities, I have been able to anticipate His movement and be bold in situations that previously would have made me nervous. Awareness of our spiritual gift allows us to take on a warrior stance in the midst of spiritual battles because we know what weapon we are picking up for the fight.

It is important to understand that spiritual gifts are distinct from our natural talents and abilities. As we have already discussed, our talents, abilities, and natural interests play a role in understanding our purpose. Spiritual gifts are, by definition, enlivened by the Holy Spirit. It is important not to glory in the gift but rather to delight in the One who gives the gift. Operating in our spiritual giftedness will always happen in a spirit of humility and yielding to the Holy Spirit. If we are operating in a spirit of pride or self-interest, then any power we wield is not aligned with our God-given purpose.

This pitfall, however, is not a reason to resist learning and growing in our gift. We should not confuse God operating in spite of us to be akin to being alive to our spiritual giftedness and moving toward our purpose. The Old Testament story of Balaam's donkey stands as a warning to us in case we operate in presumption about our purpose. In this story, Ballam is determined to go to Moab even after God has explicitly instructed him not to. As he saddled his donkey and prepared to pursue his path out of personal will, the Angel of the Lord stood in the road, sword in hand, and opposed forward progress. Balaam was blinded by his personal ambition, maybe even reasoning that he had given his word that he would show up in Moab and tried to carry on. His donkey could see the Angel and resisted movement in spite of the whipping he experienced from his master. Miraculously, the donkey spoke to Balaam, reasoning with Balaam to reconsider his actions and turn back from his personal plan (Numbers 22:1-41). The donkey is evidence that God can use anyone or anything to deliver his message and divert us from a reckless path. However, may we not desire to be the donkey, an unaware and unlikely participant in God's plan. We should yield and listen to the direction of God's voice, aware that He is near and wants to use us.

In my own life, there is not much more gratifying than to see God's Spirit move in my story to touch the life of another person. Sometimes I find myself stupefied, feeling more like an observer than an active participant when God chooses to enliven my gifts in service of someone else. As I have grown in my awareness of my gifts and look-back over the course of my life I can see which gifts have been most prominent. Also, it is important to share that I believe that God expands the gifts that we have as we use the ones He gives. I know that God has gifted me with exhortation, wisdom and administration. I know these are gifts of the spirit because I hear the feedback over and over when I share encouragement that it has a strengthening impact on the inner person. When I listen intently to someone who is in a sticky situation, it is natural for me to be able to express discerned insight aligned to scriptural truth. It is often said back to me that my counsel is grounded in wisdom. These are not gifts I can manufacture myself, rather it is evidence of God's spirit activating toward the common good of others. I get to be the vessel He uses. Because spiritual gifts are not something we can manufacture ourselves, rather they are abilities that the Holy Spirit endows, it is often a communally evident gift.

As we grow in awareness of our spiritual gifts, we can more readily tune in when God is seeking to use us to encourage or equip others. We will see the nudges from the Holy Spirit as opportunities to meet a need rather than as a dare to take a risk. Several groups have curated spiritual gifts and resources to help believers discover their giftedness. Feel free to look up your own by searching for "best spiritual gifts test" in your search engine (https://giftstest.com/).

Once you have taken a test or reviewed the list, it is important to validate and verify what others experience when they are with you. The first verifying action is to pray about the results. Ask God to make it clear to you which gift or gifts He has given to you. It isn't God's desire that we should be unaware of the gift He has given. The second way we can confirm our gifts is through community. We know that when we get together with other Christians, God is active among us. Therefore, it is most likely that your gifts have been impactful to others if you are active in any type of gathering of believers. Ask your local community of believers which of the spiritual gifts have you seen active in me? Finally, reflect on your experiences. Where have you experienced deep joy in serving others? Often, this joy is indicative of our spiritual gifts. While all of us have a responsibility to give, those with the gift of giving will experience deep joy as they give, even when it is risky. Similarly, while we are all called to serve and be hospitable, those with the gift of service or hospitality will experience deep satisfaction in the opportunity to be in the background, creating experiences for others.

It is also relevant to note that Paul urges us to grow in the gifts, meaning that God will give us additional gifts to be used in service to His kingdom mission. That said, start with what He has already operationalized in you.

- What are the spiritual gifts you think you have?

_____

_____

_____

_____

- Ask 3-5 people who know you from church or a small group to help identify your spiritual gifts.

  _____

  _____

  _____

  _____

- Read the lists of gifts in Romans 12 and 1 Corinthians 12. Highlight the ones that jump out to you, or you have seen God activate in you.

  _____

  _____

  _____

  _____

- Reflect, can you remember a time when God seemed to move in you to meet the spiritual, physical, or emotional needs of others? What was that experience? Do you see any of the gifts listed in the above passages at work in that story?

  _____

  _____

  _____

  _____

  _____

  _____

  _____

## Prayer:

God, thank You for the opportunity to serve Your Church through Spirit-empowered gifts. Will You please help me to see the gifts You have given me?

## Physical Characteristics

Our physical bodies are designed for our purpose. This includes our physical abilities, our minds, and what energizes and drains us. Everyone knows a child who has dreams and desires to become a professional athlete but doesn't have the physical characteristics to support that dream. Likewise, it seems that some individuals were born to race, jump, or play professional sports. Some people have naturally interesting voices, born to be on the radio. Others are born with striking beauty. There is no physical characteristic, whether lovely or less desirable, that is outside the purpose of God. God uses our physical characteristics to support our purpose.

In the Gospel of John in the ninth chapter, there is a story told of a blind man who happened to be nearby when Jesus and his disciples were passing his village doing ministry. In verses 1-4, it states, "As he went along, he saw a man, blind from birth. His disciples asked him, 'Rabbi, who sinned, this man or his parents, that he was born blind?' Jesus answered them, 'Neither this man nor his parents sinned but this happened so that the works of God might be displayed in him.'" Immediately following this statement, Jesus heals the man by spitting in the mud and putting it on his eyes. This man's physical characteristics were the canvas for Jesus' miracle lesson that day.

It is interesting to me that the disciples assumed that the blind man's physical condition was somehow a consequence for something he or his parents had done. In their ancient worldview, a physical limitation such as blindness could have no redeeming value; they concluded it must be a divine punishment. It was not, in their estimation, a design feature. While it is tempting to assume that we have progressed so much in our worldview, I'm afraid many modern thinkers draw the same conclusion when we see our own limitations or differences. We even refer to some of our physical characteristics as disabilities. However, what this passage is teaching us is that what we see as a barrier to living a meaningful life may actually be how God plans to intersect our stories at just the right time. While physical healing may not be His plan, we can be confident that God doesn't waste or create in vain.

Nic Vujicic is a motivational speaker and evangelist. He travels the world speaking on large stages to spread his message of hope. He shares how obstacles, specifically physical obstacles, may actually be opportunities in disguise. Nic has no arms or legs. Nic's parents were given no medical explanation for why their little baby boy was born with this condition. We now know that this is called tetra-amelia syndrome, a rare condition that affects 1 out of every 71,000 pregnancies. While to most, this would be devastating news, Nic's early life felt quite despairing. He even shared that, at one point, he tried to commit suicide. However, he was saved and began to contribute meaningfully to others. At age 17, he began speaking to church groups and is now known as a leading speaker on the power of resilience and reframing your mind.

It would be easy to conclude that because of physical limitations, Nic's purpose would be inhibited. However, he was able to see God's vision for him. What others would view as an obstacle, Nic transformed into an opportunity. Whatever our physical abilities or perceived disabilities, God is looking for a willingness to offer our bodies to Him. In Romans 12:1, Paul urges us to "offer your bodies as living sacrifices to God." Our energies should be given back to God as a vehicle to achieve His purpose. Whether we perceive those bodies to be beautiful, strong, incomplete or defective, our bodies are the place in which we inhabit our purpose. They are more than a means to an end. They are an offering that we present back to God, asking, "How do You want to use this gift? How should I use my energies for Your glory?"

While most of us don't have stories as dramatic as Nic or the man born blind, our bodies have various features and flaws. God intends to use our bodies as both delivery mechanisms for living out our purpose and as messengers. Our bodies are the way that we complete the work he has prepared for us, as told in Ephesians 2:10. While Nic and the blind man are both brilliant examples of God using physical limitations (as we might label them), God also has a purpose for our most desirable physical characteristics. This includes external features such as height, beauty, or athleticism. Sometimes these types of features can be seen as some sort of cosmic lottery or genetic privilege. While there is certainly science to support the role that DNA plays in helping form our physical features, there is also a spiritual reality that God is intentional in the way we are knit together. What this means is we can view our physical characteristics as something to explore with God rather than something to boast in or hide.

God plans to deploy His plan through our physical bodies to achieve the good work ahead of us. "Work," in the scientific sense, is defined as energy transfer. One of the key things that our body tells us is what energizes and drains us. Our body is designed, through our nervous system, to communicate what is good and life-giving versus what is negative or draining. "The purpose of the human body is to facilitate the body's energy pathway (energy input, energy storage, work output, and heat release) in order to maintain the conditions necessary for life and allow you to accomplish those things which are important to you." The body is both a vehicle for our purpose and a communication system.

Similar to a vehicle, our internal systems will send us signals to pay attention or "check the engine light," if you will. Our bodies are made up of billions of neurons loaded with messages. These neurons signal to our bodies and help us understand the impact of different activities on our overall system. Our bodies help us understand which work or activities are suitable for us to perform and which work will burn us out. Different individuals who are wired up for external stimulation may notice that large group activities or loaded schedules leave them buzzing. While individuals wired for depth may find themselves retreating to an internal mental space. Design features inform how we should steward our energy or work toward our purpose.

Lack of acknowledgement of our physical bodies in the discussion of purpose is functionally dualism. The fact that Jesus himself inhabited a physical body should indicate that our bodies are good and that God intends to activate our lives inside of, rather than apart from, our physical bodies. We know from 1 Corinthians 6:19 that God considers our body to be a dwelling place for the Holy Spirit. It stands to reason, then, that we should consider what abilities or disabilities God may have crafted in accordance with His plan for us. In addition, we need to ask, what messages did He intend to send us through the physical structuring of our bodies that impact our purpose on earth? How is it that the Holy Spirit plans to use our bodies to accomplish the fulfillment of God's kingdom on earth?

Saint Theresa of Avila said, "Christ has no body on earth but yours. Yours are the eyes with which he looks compassionately on this world. Your feet are the feet with which he walks to do good. Your hands are the hands with which he blesses the world. Christ has no body on earth now except yours." Let that sink in for a second. Not only is your physical body important in helping you understand those things that you are designed to do…it is now also the main vehicle through which God's purposes will be achieved on the planet. God can use anyone and anything to achieve His plans. Believers. Non-believers. Rocks. Donkeys. However, God desires to use our surrendered bodies to experience His work in us. We are not spirits with bodies. We are vessels of the Holy Spirit who exist to meet the needs of the world. Your body, perceived flaws and all, is meant to be a purpose-driven figure poised to host the Spirit of God among the people with whom you live, work, and play.

This personal example is probably a little more personal than I prefer, but if you have read this far, I'm going to consider you a friend. I'm the oldest sister of two younger sisters. Also, my first professional job was supervising a housing facility for 200 freshmen women at a small, private liberal arts college. It was during this time that God really highlighted for me the importance of physical characteristics. I had over-spiritualized God's interest in my development to primarily be concerned with my heart and my moral choice-making. However, it became clear to me, as a young professional, how profoundly God cared about my body as a part of my overall expression of purpose.

Since we are close now, I will tell you my age. I was a teenager in the 90s and graduated high school in the year 2000. During that period of time, diet culture and eating disorders were an unfortunate trend. I got caught up in that trend during the

"Clueless" era of 1996. During my 8th grade year, I developed an eating disorder. As a natural result, I began to lose weight and consequently got positive affirmation for what I looked like. Never mind that I was subsisting on iceberg lettuce and fat-free ranch dressing. I *looked* great. The 90s were a time obsessed with being thin and beautiful. Niki Taylor and other flawless Cover Girls graced the pages of Seventeen magazine. As is still the case, young girls are the prime target for this kind of messaging. I wanted to be beautiful, and thin was beautiful. So, I starved myself. Peppermints, water, and walking. That was my routine to support my goals. Even the church ladies commented about how great I looked *now*. It felt great, so I kept on. Control. Attention. Affirmation. Mostly fueled by an ideal image and an unhealthy dose of self-loathing. I'm not sure my parents knew where my mind and body were. It is normal to thin out as you grow.

The main thing that shook me out of that habit was running cross country. I quickly realized that in order to run, I needed to eat. I began eating and running and mostly right-sized my relationship with food and exercise. However, I didn't really heal my mindset toward the nutrition/appearance dynamic until I understood the tight relationship that existed between how I talked about myself and the influence I held over my sisters and other younger girls who looked up to me. I remember walking down the hall while I was at my job supervising freshmen residents. The Lord spoke to me loud and clear. He pointed out the responsibility I had to be a healthy example of someone who accepted their body and appearance as the gift that it is. How I accepted myself was going to have a trickle-down impact on the way others did or didn't accept themselves. If I didn't learn to value the body God had given me, I would be stunted in my purpose. What I heard God say to me was, "I made you beautiful on purpose." As I write this, it nearly stops me as hard as it did that day. It is a little embarrassing even now to type those words because I don't consider myself to be outstandingly beautiful. But God does. Up to that point, I didn't see physical beauty as something that God had a point of view on. Rather, I had accepted society's voice as the only perspective in the conversation. That day, God helped me understand that nothing he does is by accident. There isn't anything he has given me that isn't an asset he intends to use for his glory. Offering up our bodies as instruments for God's purpose is an essential way of walking in his plan for us.

Questions to ask yourself about design:

- What activities energize or drain you?

_____

_____

_____

_____

_____

- What skills or roles do you find yourself uniquely good at?

_____

_____

_____

_____

_____

- What do people who know you well say you are best at?

  _____

  _____

  _____

  _____

  _____

- Are there any aspects of your physical body that feel like a flaw rather than a feature?

  _____

  _____

  _____

  _____

  _____

- How does your physical body serve your designed abilities?

  _____

  _____

  _____

  _____

  _____

## Prayer:

God, I know that You have given me abilities and a physical body to help me live out Your plan for me on earth. Help me see those things that are unique about my physical body that are indicative of my purpose.

# CHAPTER 5

# DESIRES

"The line of life is a ragged diagonal between
duty and desire."
—William R. Alger

D esires are what we wish in our hearts was reality. Growing up, my view of Christian desire was malformed by a theology that depicted desire as bad, something that would lead you away from your God-given purpose. It went something like this: "The heart is deceptive, therefore, our desires, coming from our heart, are there to trick us into following Satan rather than Jesus." Essentially, if you want something, you need to kill that desire as fast as you can before it takes you in the wrong direction. While it is true that un-surrendered desire can lead us astray, Jesus is not against our desires. I will say that again. Jesus is not against our desires. In fact, Jesus *cares* about our desires. Our desires are powerful indicators of our purpose and motivations. We actually need our desires intact, as God created them, to help us maintain momentum to pursue our purpose.

God-given desires feel like soul sparks—moments that ignite the pilot light of our inner purpose. In *Sacred Romance*, John Eldredge highlights how desires propel us forward and warns of the dark forces that benefit from our loss of desire. "One of the most poisonous of all Satan's whispers is simply, 'Things will never change,'" he writes. This lie kills expectation, trapping our hearts in the present. To keep desire alive, we must nurture a vision for what lies ahead. Jesus promised to "make all things new," and though we can't fully imagine what God has planned, we're called to dream boldly, for desire thrives through imagination—the antidote to resignation.

It's striking that the enemy of our soul would work to dismantle our desires, showing just how powerful they are in God's design. Rather than dismissing desires, perhaps we should see them as vital signposts, revealing the unique path God has set before us.

As we touched on earlier in the purpose formula, neuroscience, and psychology reveal that desire is a more potent motivator than discipline. While discipline—what we feel we *have* to do—can drive short-term action, it's desire—what we *want* to do—that taps into the brain's emotional center, creating a lasting, intrinsic motivation that helps us reach a state of flow. When we act from desire, we're energized and focused, naturally engaging in work that resonates deeply within us.

Our desires are as unique as the colors on an artist's palette, each one blending to form a distinct expression of purpose. Rather than forcing ourselves to fit a rigid mold, our desires give shape to the path we're uniquely designed to walk. In this way, our desires don't just drive us; they guide us toward a life that is deeply personal, purposeful, and fulfilling.

The science around motivation taps into the role that desires play in our willingness to pursue anything. Dopamine is the brain chemical most associated with pleasure. Prior to doing research, I assumed that dopamine was the thing that we get after we do something enjoyable. However, the reality is that dopamine is the reward chemical that inspires us to pursue any given thing. Dopamine, basing its information on past experiences and relatable patterns, gives us the motivation to do things that will give us pleasure. Basically, dopamine precedes the active pursuit of things we will love based on things we have loved.

According to the Cleveland Clinic, dopamine is a "chemical messenger, communicating messages between nerve cells in your brain and the rest of your body." Dopamine is responsible for so many functions in our body, including movement, memory, motivation, attention, and mood. When we overstimulate our brain through stress or highly rewarding, low-effort behaviors (i.e. social media scrolling, video games, porn, etc.), we can disorient our dopamine receptors. This can create untrustworthy desires. Impaired dopamine receptors don't act as the trusty indicators they are designed to be. However, when functioning properly, these brain chemicals support the enduring pursuit of a healthy, purpose-driven life.

The presence of dopamine is an indicator that God wants us to want things. The key is to understand the patterns of desire that God has imprinted on our hearts. By loving Him, we ensure that our system stays open to delightful desires and experiences. The Psalmist encourages us to "Delight yourself in the Lord, and he will give you the desires of your heart" (Psalm 37:4, ESV). We know our desires become clarified in their intended form and become trustworthy messengers of our purpose when we delight in Him.

We don't always know what to do with desire. It can feel uncontrollable. According to vulnerability researcher, Brené Brown "Joy is the most vulnerable emotion we experience." Instead of basking in joy, sometimes we self-sabotage. Self-sabotage is when we act in a way that interrupts our ability to be healthy or achieve the goals we set for ourselves. We are afraid of desire and what it means, so we numb ourselves to take away the discomfort of admitting that we want things. Opening ourselves to desire brings the inherent risk of being disappointed and, in extreme cases, even devastated by those unmet desires. As a means of protection, we deny or ignore our desires. Numbing can take many forms. My belief system drove me to deny desire, a form of numbing. Eating, shopping, scrolling, distraction…I could go on. All of these activities can turn into numbing activities because they are low-risk reward behaviors that allow us to feel better without pursuing the things we really want. We avoid doing the work to get what we want. This avoidance is often subconscious for many of us.

We should not fear, hate, or ignore our desires, as they help us uncover our God-given purpose. The corruption of desires that we have experienced and willfully committed should not lead us to the conclusion that desire is bad. Rather, the scriptures and our physical bodies would cause us to conclude that perhaps God intends to use our desires as a means of finding our purpose. We must acknowledge that our numbing tendencies are Trojan horses. We cannot allow the sneaky habits of distraction to lull us to sleep and thereby miss the calling that is on our lives.

We see David crying out and being raw about mingled pain and desire. In Psalm 38:9 (ESV), he cries out, "Oh Lord, my every desire is before You; my groaning is not hidden from you. My heart pounds, my strength fails, and even the light of my eyes has faded." He is in a battle, and he recognizes that his desires matter to God. He doesn't hide or numb them; rather, he lays them before God even as he is painfully struggling. His wholehearted willingness to bring his pain to the Lord allows him to be satisfied even as he is not yet restored. He recognized the role that his emotions, desires, and pain played in his ability to be fully alive.

Brené Brown states, "We cannot selectively numb our emotions, when we numb the painful emotions, we also numb the positive ones." I do not mean to conflate emotions and desires. They are distinct but related. We are designed to experience emotions as we realize and recognize our desires. This is why both pain and joy are connected to the ability to see our God-given desires.

If King David had picked up the same theology that my young heart misunderstood, he might have dutifully and in a spirit of discouragement returned to the battle. He may have tried to rally his men with half of his heart because he didn't know that God actually wanted to interface with his desires. God wanted him to lead his kingdom wholeheartedly. Had King David presumed that God didn't care, or worse, that desires were evil, he might have taken a "suck it up" attitude back to the battle and been a begrudging soldier rather than an inspiring war hero. It is hard to say what the outcome would have been; we can only imagine. God gave him the capacity to maintain access to his heart, which was a critical element of his leadership ability. We know King David as a man after God's heart, fully alive and full of desire.

He is also the perfect case study for the distinction between sin and desire. While our desires can lead us astray, they do not have to. In the first chapter of James, we read, "Each person is tempted when they are dragged away by their own evil desires." When I read this as a teenager, I thought, 'Aha!' there it is again, our dirty, evil, ugly desires. I better get rid of those! I hadn't lined up the other texts that verify that desires have a holy and an evil capacity. We see in this passage that James offers a qualifier. We are dragged away by our 'evil' desires. Evil desires give birth to sin. Holy desires give birth to love.

In the story of King David, we see evil desires activated in the story of Bathsheba. We know that he should have been at war (2 Samuel 11), but he stayed behind, sending his army ahead of him. The rest of the story is that while at home, he sends for a married woman, impregnates her, and ends up murdering her husband. Growing up, I viewed his lust for Bathsheba as evidence that desire itself is something to fear. Look at the righteous King David, pulled down by his desires. Everyone knows that lust is an evil desire, and it must have the animalistic power to manipulate actions. As we explore the passage further, it is notable that King David is no victim of desire. His choice to satisfy lust is a sinful expression of the legitimate desire for comfort and belonging that he wrongly met through transactional sexual satisfaction. Peering closer, if we trace the origin of this desire, we see that the evil desire that gave birth to lust was the desire for comfort instead of responsibility. It was his decision to stay home, presumably because he felt entitled to do so, that led him down a pathway that led to sin. What we see in this story is misplaced desire and ravenous appetites. If he had embraced righteous desire, the story would have ended much differently.

A righteous desire for responsibility can be described as a deep, ethical drive to take ownership of one's actions, contributions, and commitments, motivated by integrity and a commitment to serve others. It's a desire rooted in purpose, not power; it comes from a place of wanting to make a positive impact, foster trust, and uphold the well-being of others. This kind of responsibility transcends mere duty or obligation; it's about aligning one's strengths, values, and actions to benefit the greater good, even when challenges arise.

At its core, this desire involves a willingness to be accountable and a readiness to steward resources, relationships, and influence in a way that reflects humility and honor. It is fueled by an understanding that true responsibility enriches not only the individual but the entire community or organization they serve. We know that King David had many instances of demonstrating his righteous desires.

One powerful example of King David embracing his responsibility as king is found in the story of his leadership during the battle against the Philistines, specifically when he faced Goliath (1 Samuel 17). Although David was young and not yet king, this moment reveals his profound sense of responsibility to defend his people—a responsibility he would carry into his reign as king. When the Israelites faced Goliath, a giant Philistine warrior who struck fear into the entire Israelite army, David stepped forward, motivated not by personal gain but by a desire to protect Israel and honor God. David said, "The Lord who delivered me from the paw of the lion and from the paw of the bear will deliver me from the hand of this Philistine" (1 Samuel 17:37, ESV). Here, he exemplifies righteous responsibility, trusting in God and willing to place himself in danger for the sake of his people's safety.

Another example from later in his reign is when David led his army personally in battle, showing a king's commitment to stand alongside his people. Even though his advisors later urged him to stay back for his own safety, David's willingness to engage in battles and serve on the front lines demonstrates his deep sense of duty to his nation and his understanding that a righteous leader is not only a figure of authority but also a servant prepared to make sacrifices for his people. In these moments, David's actions reflect the role righteous desires play in helping us live our purpose, as David chooses courage, humility, and service over comfort, showing his commitment to God and his people.

David is a great test case for demonstrating the beauty of desire and the destructive role that feeding the wrong desires can play. In Galatians 5, we find a profound lesson on appetites and desires. Paul reminds us that what we feed will grow. If we continually indulge sinful desires, our appetite for sin only strengthens, leading us further away from God's purpose. But if we choose to feed our spiritual desires, our hunger for God and His righteousness grows, drawing us nearer to Him. This concept of "reaping what we sow" underscores a simple truth: our appetites and desires are not meant to be suppressed or eliminated. Instead, they are tools—mechanisms for living by God's standards—meant to guide us toward lives that reflect His love and righteousness.

Desires, especially righteous ones, hold a vital place in our spiritual journey. They are not obstacles to be overcome but instruments to be carefully cultivated. Just as a righteous desire for responsibility compels us to serve and steward with integrity, our spiritual hunger can direct us toward a deeper relationship with God. In this way, our desires become aligned with God's purpose, helping us live in ways that honor Him and serve others.

When we recognize that our desires can be directed toward something greater, we see that they are not inherently flawed or sinful. Rather, they are opportunities—soul-level inclinations meant to pull us toward our purpose in God. Feeding these desires with spiritual practices, community, and acts of service helps them flourish in righteousness. Like any good gardener, we are called to nurture our spiritual appetites, letting them grow so that they bear fruit for God's kingdom and allow us to live with courage, humility, and a deep, guiding sense of purpose.

When desire is rightly viewed, desire is essential to living a full life in Christ. God designed our bodies to utilize desire as a messenger to our whole system to pursue the purpose He has for us. We must lead ourselves well, being fully aware of the way we numb ourselves and the impact of distractions. Evil desires dissuade us from pursuing our God-given passions. We must purify our hearts and minds and renew them as we are encouraged, "Do not conform to the pattern of this world, but be transformed by the renewing of your mind. Then you will be able to test and approve what God's will is—his good, pleasing and perfect will" (Romans 12:1-2). A healthy mind and heart lead to pure and good thoughts and actions.

Perhaps a better spiritual lesson would have been to feed holy desire. Cultivate a healthy appetite. Don't destroy your ability to desire at all. In order to recover desire, it may be necessary to remember ourselves as children. Kids have an incredible knack for generating and sustaining high levels of desire. Their hearts leap at novel experiences, and their minds are endlessly curious about peculiar things. Just as Jesus invited His disciples to become like children, we can glean a bit of wisdom from the way our hearts responded to joy before we learned to harden ourselves against it. Desires are often those things in which we find profound fascination. As children, we often have a mysterious curiosity about certain topics. It can be as simple as a love of trains or dinosaurs or a love of reading. We learn to suppress our desire early on as we're taught to shed them as we mature. However, if we look at great scientists, inventors, or even uniquely successful business people, teachers, or ministers, their profound fascination typically stems from childhood.

One such cultural icon who marked the world with his profound fascination is Walt Disney. In a study of his early life and career, we learn that Walt was marked by an early fascination with drawing. In fact, he was so preoccupied with drawing that he was entranced by his creations. His grade school teachers assumed that he was intellectually challenged. His artistic interest turned into obsession. His pursuit was relentless in the field of animation. The advent of Mickey Mouse, an international symbol, was one of his greatest contributions to the world. Nearly one hundred years ago, Mickey Mouse splashed onto the scene, eventually becoming the most notable cartoon of all time and a beloved image representing happiness and magic. To his own account, Walt Disney would say that Mickey Mouse and the creation of Disneyland in California were the truest manifestations of his desire. It was through his dedication to excellence and desire to draw that he was able to shape the dreams and memories of countless other illustrators, children, and families who benefit from his contributions.

Like Walt's desire to animate, childhood dreams are often one of the earliest forms of desire. Nearly as soon as a child is old enough to dream, we start asking him this question, "What do you want to be when you grow up?" The intent of the question is to tap into that child's heart and mind. What do they imagine for themselves? The answers are always diverse. A fireman. Police officer. A teacher. An artist. A doctor. The answers reveal that we do not all have the same dream. In fact, I believe that dreams are evidence of God working ahead of time to lead us to our destiny. While we may not ever create something of global impact, our dreams are relevant windows into our soul.

Jo Saxton asks the following questions in her book, *The Dream of You*, "What was the dream you had of yourself from the very beginning? Before life interrupted, before anyone told you what you were allowed to be?" **Before people told you what you were allowed to be.** Let that phrase sink in for just one minute. Some of our early dreams were not received with curiosity or openness. Sometimes, we did not have the language to navigate what appeared to be barriers blocking our pursuit of that dream. So, we settle for lesser dreams. Mistakenly assuming that those childhood dreams were nothing more than childish fantasy. However, for most, there are themes in those dreams that are still alive and sometimes functioning inside. Saxton goes on to say, "The dream of you is God's vision of you, your real, true identity, and your God-given purpose." If God dreams of you, perhaps it is ok to tap into the seeds of desire He planted all of those years ago. Maybe we can learn to listen to the themes of our desires that have been echoing throughout our lives, telling the story of God's intended purpose.

Our early desires might be clues to our truest desires. Perhaps the little boy who dreamed of being a police officer wasn't hoping for power and control but had a heart of justice and to see things made right in the world. Maybe the little girl who wanted to be a singer wasn't seeking fame but has a message to share with the world. What about you? What do your early dreams tell you about your heart's truest desires? It is important that you can answer the question, "What do I most desire?"

When influential voices in my life challenged me with the piercing question: "Jessica, what do you want?" Though simple, I remember feeling caught off guard by it. At the time, I was deeply engaged in meaningful work at the university, certain that my role in Christian Higher Education was a natural fit for my skills and passions. I loved Jesus, loved learning, and found joy in guiding students toward their future. Even on the hardest days, I felt the purpose in my work. Yet, the question continued to echo: *What do you want?* Unable to answer, I turned to prayer: "God, I may not know what I want, but You do. Will You show me?"

As I took a leap of faith into the business world, I was not confident that I would find success. But I was confident that He was leading me toward the full life that He had promised. Shakily, I followed the signals and began to do the work that was in front of me, and slowly, my heart began to beat again. I remembered the dream I had as a child to be a pastor and to influence people toward truth. Each day, though without using the language of Christian subculture, I was given unbelievable opportunities to help leaders with clarity and wisdom. I was sitting in rooms and hearing stories that my old position would not have allowed me to experience. I began to uncover desires and talents in other people that had been buried and numbed just like mine. I had to bring life to the people I was serving. My desire was awakened and so was the joy I had for the work in front of me.

I want to close this section with an acknowledgment that it is tempting to be general about desire, but I want you to be specific. Your specific desires are the pathfinder lights that illuminate where God wants you to contribute. I remember talking with a student who was deeply frustrated—even angry—that the university wasn't rallying around the issue of homelessness in OKC. This was the core issue he cared most about. He believed that if everyone truly cared about God and people, they'd take immediate, collective action to address it. While his passion was admirable, it sparked an important realization in me: each of us is uniquely drawn to different causes and that diversity in our convictions is no accident—it's an essential part of God's design. Only God is able to care deeply and specifically about all the needs in the world. He has already created a plan to meet those needs. His plan is us, living our lives on purpose, for a purpose.

Imagine if we all cared about the same issue; so many needs would go unmet. Just as a body has many parts, each with a specific purpose, our individual passions equip us to address a range of challenges. One person may be driven to fight injustice, another to improve mental health access, and yet another to protect the environment. God gives each of us specific burdens and gifts, not to unify our focus on one issue but to ensure that, together, we can serve a broader spectrum of needs. Rather than expecting everyone to mobilize around the same cause, we can honor the variety of callings among us. This diversity is precisely how God intends to meet the needs of the world.

In his book *Practicing the Way*, John Mark Comer talks about the heart of God toward the needs of the world. His insight is helpful in that he points us to our particular role in reflecting the heart of God to the world. He says, "God's heart is universal, literally it is for all of the universe. Our hearts are not universal. We're finite, mortal, a vapor. But on each of us, Jesus will lay one small part of his universal heart of love. We will find our hearts drawn to particular justice issues, people groups, neighbor families, or lines of work and it will feel like joy."

God literally cares about everything at the same time with particular love, and He is not overwhelmed. However, we are not designed with that same capacity. We are designed with limited ability to make a difference. And in proportion to our abilities, God has given each of us a unique and holy opportunity to care about, love, and work toward a piece of His kingdom coming on earth. Our desires are windows for how He wants us to love the world. "And it will feel like joy."

Questions to uncover desire:

- What activities do you drift toward when there are no responsibilities attached?

  _____

  _____

  _____

  _____

- What brings you joy?

  _____

  _____

  _____

  _____

- What world issue deeply upsets you?

  _____

  _____

  _____

  _____

- What did you always dream of becoming?

  _____

  _____

  _____

  _____

- How do you see those desires show up in your life right now?

_____

_____

_____

_____

- What contribution would you most like to make to your world?

_____

_____

_____

_____

## Prayer:

Lord, give me a clean heart. Help me see the holy desires You placed inside of me. Help me to see any evil desires that are leading me astray, and give me a heart of wisdom to see the difference. I want to be fully alive, desiring the things You desire. Take this heart of stone and give me a beating heart of flesh. Help me, Lord, to be fully alive with You.

## Notes:

What do you hear the Lord saying? What desires or dreams (even if they feel random) are coming to mind?

_____

_____

_____

_____

_____

_____

# CHAPTER 6

# DISAPPOINTMENTS

"If you have a 'Why' to live, you can endure
almost any 'How.'"
—Fredrich Nietzsche

Probably the most poignant but undesirable experiences that point us to our purpose are our disappointments. Disappointments are the things that break our hearts, wound us, or attach themselves to us, weighing us down. They are the rocks in our backpacks that we carry with us into all of our relationships, conversations, and responsibilities. Sometimes, disappointments are because of stupid things we have done, and other times, they are because of others' poor choices. Disappointments are no less important in helping us find our purpose than our desires. In fact, these are the broken places where others might find the deepest sense of connection with us.

Disappointment and challenge play a crucial role in developing a meaningful purpose by forcing individuals to reassess their values, goals, and priorities. When faced with disappointments or challenges, people may question their current path and seek more fulfillment and purpose in their lives. These difficult situations can push individuals out of their comfort zones and prompt them to explore new possibilities and passions. Adversity can also lead to personal growth and resilience as individuals learn to persevere in the face of obstacles and setbacks. Overall, disappointment and challenge can inspire individuals to pursue a more meaningful purpose by encouraging self-reflection, growth, and a deeper understanding of what truly matters to them.

In the opening chapter of 2 Corinthians, Paul actually sees heartbreak as a purposeful tool for us to uncover our purpose. In fact, disappointment may be the Swiss Army knife of tools for discovery. In this passage, we first see that God meets us in our disappointment. He brings us comfort where we need it. The passage reads: "Praise be to the God and Father of our Lord Jesus Christ, the Father of compassion and the God of all comfort, who comforts us in all our troubles, so that we can comfort those in any trouble with the comfort we ourselves receive from God" (2 Corinthians 1:3-4).

God pours the triumphant, healing blood of Jesus into our broken places, telling the story of hope and purpose. That event or disappointment that we thought might kill us has now become God's tool for His glory. Rather than shame, we have hope and healing. The world is desperately hoping for a story that speaks life into their broken places. The double blessing of disappointment is that because we have been comforted, we get to be the vessel of hope for others.

There is a Japanese art form called "kintsugi" that is translated as "Golden" (Kin) "Joinery" (Tsugui). In this art form, crushed metals such as gold, silver, or platinum are mixed with lacquer and used to fix broken pottery. The liquid gold is infused into the broken places to achieve what is known as the "Golden Repair." As a philosophy, it treats breakage and repair as part of the history of an object rather than something to disguise. Not only is there no attempt to hide the damage, but the repair is literally illuminated. Kintsugi is unique because it transforms brokenness into beauty rather than attempting to disguise or erase flaws. Unlike conventional repair methods, which aim to restore an item to its original state, kintsugi celebrates the object's history, emphasizing its fractures as part of its narrative. The use of precious metals makes the repair visible and valuable, turning cracks into intricate designs that enhance the piece's aesthetic and uniqueness.

This art form also embodies a philosophical perspective that contrasts with many Western ideas of perfection. Kintsugi reflects *wabi-sabi*, the Japanese appreciation for imperfection and impermanence, encouraging us to see beauty in the transience and vulnerability of life. *Wabi-sabi* is a Japanese aesthetic and philosophical concept that finds beauty in imperfection, impermanence, and simplicity. At its core, wabi-sabi celebrates the authenticity and rawness of natural, transient things rather than polished, flawless forms. It emphasizes that nothing in life is permanent, perfect, or complete, and it encourages acceptance of this reality. Every kintsugi piece becomes a one-of-a-kind artifact, bearing marks of both its fragility and resilience. This philosophy—embracing flaws as a part of wholeness—makes kintsugi not just an art form but a powerful symbol of healing, transformation, and renewal.

This art form is such a beautiful parallel to the work of God in our lives. Unlike us, God is not ashamed of our broken places. He does not hold standards of perfection that exist outside of himself. Rather, he takes the weak and broken places of our lives and performs his own golden repair. Our broken places are joined with the perfect nature of Christ through precious and imperishable grace. We have his perfect righteousness imputed into our demolished souls. Where we were weak and fragmented, he is strong and gleaming. He desires to make the jagged and cracked places of our lives a lustrous display of His glory. Our damaged places are His opportunity to perform a golden repair. It begs the question, if God is not ashamed of our broken places, then why are we? Could it be Western ideas of perfectionism that don't have a place in the kingdom of God?

Our broken places, whether physical, mental, emotional, or spiritual, whether done by us or done to us, God desires to make a golden joinery of those broken places. The very thing we felt could destroy us becomes a useful, illuminated aspect of our lives to bring hope, life, encouragement, and healing into the lives of others. When healed, our disappointments dig wells of compassion that produce purposeful wisdom and comfort. Our wounds are healed, and as they shine forth, we invite others to do the same.

## My Golden Repair

I went to college to be a missionary. In my mind, a missionary was someone who lived out their faith in Jesus at the most sacrificial level. Only the most serious Christians would live their lives this way. From this framework, I thought that moving overseas and telling people about Jesus was the best way I could serve God and live out His purposes for me. During my freshman year of college, I started struggling with dark depression. It was due to a storm of reasons, including doing too much, not sleeping enough, and walking down a path of shameful choices that caused me to question my values and worthiness. By the end of the summer and leading into my sophomore year of college, I found myself suicidal and despondent. I vividly remember the day I was driving my car home from church and feeling like it was a very logical decision to try to crash my car and cause my own death.

I wish I could say that was an eye-opener, but I continued to struggle even as I sought professional help. Through a series of interventions that included medication, counseling, resting, reading my Bible, and intentionally slowing down, I found my way back to hope. I haven't visited a place as dark as that in my mind for that length of time since then. However, I hold that period of my life as a space where God truly healed me with His compassion. That experience dug deep wells of patience in my heart for people who struggle, especially with mental health and feelings of worthlessness. I understand how a "normal" person can lose hope and also know that there is a hopeful future for all of us. I see now that a person can appear to be doing well to others but inside be experiencing a different reality. That experience helped me be on the lookout for ways that I can be a conduit to see other people who may be wearing a mask of "I'm fine" while they are struggling. God used that experience to bring a purposeful determination in my heart to become someone who encourages others to find hope. God meets us in the very disappointments we think might break us. Ultimately, these things become a display for His glory.

## The Gift of Disappointment

It is common for individuals to experience a shift when disappointment or tragedy occurs. There are really only two choices, learn from the valley of the shadow of death or get stuck in the dark. When we get stuck there, we can begin to feel like life is against us, taking on a victim mentality. However, when we learn that God is with us and our life has meaning because of the disappointment, there is often a great transformation that takes place. This transformation produces resilience. This gift of healed pain can be the strength we offer. Dr. Steven Taylor is a psychologist who studies individuals who have experienced "tumultuous or traumatic" life events (i.e., cancer diagnosis, depression, addiction). His research findings suggest that some people emerge from such events transformed. "In terms of purpose, the shift has two main effects. First, people feel a much stronger sense of purpose. Second, they shift away from a personal accumulative purpose, to an altruistic and/or self-expansive purpose." While I'm sure most individuals would not choose that hardship again, they likely would not trade the transformation either. Purpose often emerges <u>because</u> of the pain, <u>not in spite of it</u>. We are able to understand the brevity of life and the opportunity to live it with purpose. I used to wonder, how would God have produced purpose in me if I had not walked through deep depression? I used to imagine life without that season. However, I treasure the golden repair as a mechanism for strength that I may not have had otherwise.

This type of transformation happened for Joni Erickson Tada. In 1976, Joni, a strong, young athlete, was swimming with friends when she dove into water that was too shallow. She was immediately rendered a quadriplegic. Prior to that day, she had been casual about her faith and asking God to intervene. She had prayed, "Do something in my life to jerk it right side up because I'm really living this life wrong." When this terrible incident happened, she said she prayed angrily, saying, "God, is this your idea of an answer to my prayer?" While her immediate response to the disappointment was like most of ours would be—bitterness and despair—she began to process her disappointment with God. She began to open her heart up like David and lay her complaints and despair before Him. As she did, her sadness began to transform into peace and eventually, purpose. She said that what she gained was better than she could have imagined, "A deeper healing...a healing of the soul. Pushed into the arms of Jesus." "Yes, our body may be harmed...but our soul ... to find Jesus in your hell is ecstasy beyond compare and I wouldn't trade it for anything in this world."

What she noticed as she began to heal is that she had a message to share. She had experienced Jesus in a way that, prior to her accident, she had not. Because of that, she began a ministry dedicated to ensuring that people with disabilities are seen and fully participatory in the body of Christ. She is helping others. Without her disappointment and eventual golden repair, she might not have seen or been able to reach. There is nothing like disappointment turned into a positive transformation. She developed a heart of compassion to handle the suffering and needs of others. Nothing quite opens the way for the gospel like pain. When we have walked in pain, finding our purpose becomes even more significant. It builds our credibility to impact others.

Before you reflect on the way that God may have already been present in past disappointments or how he is offering you healing today, I want to give you a note of future encouragement. God is not only the healer of past or present disappointments. He is also ahead of us in our future disappointments. We can trust him to be with us when we are inevitably hurt in service to others. Self-protection from future disappointments is such a subtle killer of our ability to live out our purpose. There can be a sense that things are going okay now; God has cleaned them up, but don't want to get too comfortable because you never know when the other shoe is going to drop. This phenomenon is called, by researcher Brene Brown, "Foreboding Joy." It is the sense that something bad is going to happen even though things are going well now. I realized I was battling this sense of foreboding recently. Mentally, I was looking for escape paths from current reality, purely because I had forgotten that if the bad thing I dread does, in fact, happen, I can trust God with that future healing in the same way I have trusted him with past disappointments. God goes before us. We can trust him. He has a proven track record. Just as our discouragements point us to our sense of purpose. We can trust that God is deepening our call to walk with him in this full-life expression of purpose-driven living. We must marvel at the healer more than the healing.

Questions about disappointments:

- Where has God met you in your story, or where do you need Him to? Have you surrendered that to Him for healing?

  _____

  _____

  _____

  _____

  _____

  _____

  _____


- Are you going through something disappointing now? Ask God, "Where are you in this?"

  _____

  _____

  _____

_____

_____

_____

_____

_____

- What breaks your heart or makes you angry?

_____

_____

_____

_____

_____

- Is there any area of your life where you feel like you need to allow God to make a golden repair?

_____

_____

_____

_____

_____

_____

- Think back to a deep disappointment you have already experienced. Thinking through the lens of God's redemptive ability, what did God teach you? How has that experience strengthened you?

_____

_____

_____

_____

_____

_____

_____

## Prayer:

God, thank You for being the only One who can handle all the disappointments and wounds we endure. Thank You for being full of compassion for me. Please help me to see the way You are using my disappointments as a display of Your glory. Lord, would You help me be totally open to Your healing? Help me to be a voice of hope to others because of Your true work in me.

# CHAPTER 7

# VISION FOR IMPACT

"Your circumstances are not the problem. Your perception
of your circumstances is the problem."
—Graham Cooke

We will not see for ourselves what God can see for us. Furthermore, our sense of timeliness is often out of sync with God's timeline. The story of Joseph is a great example of someone who was able to live with a sense of purpose regardless of circumstances. Joseph was the beloved son of his father, Jacob. He was one of twelve. Scripture tells us that Jacob loved Joseph because he was born during his old age. As a token of fatherly love, Jacob had a special, colorful robe woven for his son. To his brothers, this robe was a symbol of favoritism, and it drove a pre-existing wedge between Joseph and the other eleven brothers. Scripture states that his brothers couldn't speak a kind word to Joseph because of their father's favoritism. In addition to a doting father, Joseph had special giftedness and divine presence in his life. One night, Joseph had a special dream that he and his brothers were working together to bind sheaves of wheat. Suddenly, Joseph's sheave rose above his brothers' and parents' sheaves, and correspondingly, their sheaves encircled him, bowing low. Joseph's brothers hated him all the more after he shared the dream with them. His brothers burned with jealousy and hatred that turned into plots to murder Joseph. As the brothers discussed what to do with this dreamer, they came up with a scheme that included killing Joseph and bringing his love-token coat back to their father. Knowing they would break their father's heart, the brothers agreed that Joseph had to go. Reuben, the only brother with a soft spot for Joseph, intervened and pleaded with his brothers to come up with a different way to get rid of Joseph and spare his life. Judah had just the plan. At the coaching of Judah, the brothers decided instead to sell Joseph to a group of slave traders who were headed to Egypt. We know from the rest of the chapters that Joseph did indeed survive and rise to a place of prominence in the palace, only to be thrown in prison. In prison, divine support rose again to lift Joseph once again to a place of powerful prominence where he was able to save the lives of his father and brothers during a pervasive famine (Genesis 41:9-14).

Like Joseph, we all have various experiences in our lives that shape our vision. Early on, we may naively believe that the journey to impact will be immediate or without trials. However, more often than not, we are faced with a choice. How am I going to respond to the challenge in front of me? Will I choose to be faithful to the purpose that God has placed on my life, or will I see the circumstance as preventative?

The choices we make and the experiences we have shape us. We cannot help but be influenced by our experience. However, we can choose to see what God sees, or we can choose to see what our eyes can see. When Joseph's brothers appeared before Joseph, it had been so long since they had seen him that they didn't recognize him. Joseph, however, recognized them immediately. One reason that Joseph might have been unrecognizable to them was that Joseph had been transformed spiritually, physically, and emotionally. He held no bitterness for his brothers. He held no hostility toward them for the choices they had made to reject and ruin him. Rather, we see Joseph was overwhelmed with deep emotion and responded with compassion for his brothers. When he revealed himself to his brothers, they must have been shocked. I would imagine they would have felt fear at the power Joseph had in the moment to enact revenge. However, Joseph's response to them was this:

> "'Come close to me.' When they had done so, he said, 'I am your brother Joseph, the one you sold into Egypt! And now, do not be distressed and do not be angry with yourselves for selling me here, because it was to save lives that God sent me ahead of you. For two years now there has been famine in the land, and for the next five years there will be no plowing and reaping. But God sent me ahead of you to preserve for you a remnant on earth and to save your lives by a great deliverance. So then, it was not you who sent me here, but God. He made me father to Pharaoh, lord of his entire household and ruler of all Egypt.'"
>
> Genesis 45:4-8

Joseph was transformed by his experiences. Each time he faced hardship, he was faithful with the gifts and talents that God had given him. Each time he was given an opportunity to serve, he rose in favor with his superiors because of his excellence. Joseph's times of obscurity and hardship developed him for the vision of impact that God had for him. Often, we cannot see what God hopes to do through us because our circumstances can skew our perspective. It would have been easy for Joseph to falsely assume that his dream was just a childhood fantasy. It would have been reasonable for Joseph to decide that he would protect himself from future harm that he had experienced in his family of origin. But that is not the story that his life tells. Rather, we learn from Joseph that our current and temporary circumstances may be a divine plan.

Operating in human capacity or vision distracts us from God's divine purpose for our lives. Trauma, particularly early on in our lives, has the capacity to distort our sense of purpose. Our bodies respond to stress, pressure, or worry by trying to interpret our experiences. Interpretations reside in our minds as the "stories we tell ourselves," a phrase coined by sociologist Brené Brown. These stories shape our baseline expectations for what is normal or what we should expect from a given situation next time. In fact, our brain is consistently trying to take our experiences and make them meaningful based on past experiences. Our past experiences shape our expectations and, thus, our interpretation of future experiences. This loop of interpretation and expectations is a neurobiological process by which our brains try to keep us safe and alert to stimuli. We can take hold of this process by consciously processing the meaning we are attaching to negative or positive experiences. If we are not alert, our lack of awareness can make us more skittish about taking risks or fully developing the purposes for which we are destined.

As such, it is important for us to be conscious about the experiences we are having and the meaning we assign to those experiences. What one person defines as meaningless could be a powerful event for another person. While we don't have an inside view to how Joseph processed his abandonment, enslavement, false accusations, and imprisonment, we know he did it. To overcome his brothers' rejection, he probably identified and avoided the false narratives that could have formed, clinging instead to the reality that God had a plan for his life. While he did not know the way his dreams would come to fruition, he could trust that God would make a way where it seemed to be impossible. God had a vision for impact, and because of that, he didn't need to expect doom and threat even when his circumstances would have indicated he should. We must allow ourselves to think deeply with God about our circumstances, as He is the only One who can see past what is in front of us.

James chapter 1 says, "Consider it pure joy, my brothers and sisters, whenever you face trials of many kinds because you know the testing of your faith produces perseverance. Let perseverance finish its work so that you may be mature and complete, not lacking anything." Our mindset toward difficult circumstances is critical. Our ability to endure trials gives us the perseverance we need to fully live out our divine purpose. How we interpret experiences shapes our energy, willingness, and mindset to pursue purpose. Purpose gives us eyes to see opportunities and experiences as God would have us see them. While this passage didn't exist at the time of Joseph's suffering, I can imagine him nodding in agreement. It was very likely the struggles he endured gave him the humility that it took for God to elevate him to the most powerful position in Egypt.

Early in my career, I heard it said, *"If you are not careful, your talents will take you places your character can't keep you."* Trials give us the character necessary to support the ways that God plans to deploy our purpose. While this does not mean that all of us will have a public platform, it does mean that for our lives to be deeply impactful, we must be unswayed by the philosophies of culture that would tempt us to grow bitter and hardened.

The story of our purpose is most fully told in the rearview mirror. It is often at one's funeral or later in life that we are able to see how all of the various threads of our lives have formed a tapestry of purpose. Soren Kierkegaard stated it well when he said, "Life can only be understood backwards, but it must be lived forward." Purpose is developed similarly. We can have early inklings of what we are made to do, yet it is only in the doing that those sparks become clear callings. The Adolescent Moral Development Lab at Claremont Graduate University was conducted to explore the psychology of purpose. The study discusses how purpose develops over time, typically through life experiences, role models, and opportunities for exploration. Adolescence and young adulthood are seen as critical periods for developing purpose, although it can evolve throughout life. Findings revealed that though the young people did not identify their purposes in life until later, experiences during childhood often set the stage for purposeful commitments (Bronk, 2012). Further, the age at which people tend to feel the highest sense of meaning and the lowest sense of dissatisfaction is around age 60. This may be because, at that point, individuals have come to terms with their gifts, personality, and difficulties.

It can be tempting to be discouraged in our search for purpose that we are unlikely to know the whole story as it is unfolding. We would like to skip to the last chapter to read the ending rather than being surprised or saddened by the character development that happens along the journey.

October 10, 2023, a man was exonerated for a crime he did not commit. Against a 300 year sentence, Perry James Lott had spent 31 years in prison after a wrongful conviction for the rape of a woman in Ada, Oklahoma in 1988. The evidence around the case was suspicious all along. Mr. Lott had an alibi. One of the key clues was a phone call that had taken place at the victim's place of employment. Mr. Lott didn't own a phone. What is more, he was mostly not a match for the description of the perpetrator. The only similarity was a gold tooth. In a shaky line-up, the detectives had the other individuals put gold foil over their teeth, disallowing them from opening their mouths naturally. Mr. Lott had a mustache at the time, a detail absent from the description of the perpetrator. Mr. Lott had willingly cooperated with the police's request to participate in the line-up because he didn't realize he was in trouble. It was inconceivable that he might be convicted for something he did not do. In telling his own story, Lott relates how it was outside his ability to comprehend that a jury could convict someone without a shred of evidence. Yet, they did. Nearly 30 years later, the story still evokes emotion from Lott. In his TEDX talk he says, "I was confident that the jury would release me." Lott states, "My cry of innocence went unheard." Many experts, in reviewing the case, contribute the error of justice to an overzealous prosecution, describing the entire case as an incident of misjustice. The Innocence Project worked six years to prove that this misjustice was something to overturn. Perry James Lott was eventually freed on post-conviction DNA evidence that revealed that he was in fact not the person who had committed a heinous crime in 1988.

Perry James Lott wrote a book describing his early life story and experience with wrongful conviction. In it, he does not shy away from describing the negative impact of his sentence. He finds himself mostly a stranger to life on the outside, although he is elated to be free. I remember the first time I heard Perry James Lott speak. I was part of a leadership program in our city and we were talking about criminal justice reform. As Perry Lott told his story, something stuck out to me. Peace. He had found peace in the middle of prison...an experience he should not have gone through, yet he was at peace. In his TEDX talk, with tears in his eyes, he states, "I'm no longer inmate #170167, but I'm Perry James Lott again. In closing, chew on this. I am too grateful to be hateful. If life brings you sadness, sorrow, negativity and misfortune, instead of focusing on that negativity and sadness, focus on people and places and things that bring you joy. That makes you feel a sense of peace and comfort. Focus on that and become that. As human beings, I believe that we become that which we focus on. This is not the end. My box of chocolates still continues." He has regained his identity and is free to express his purpose. He has dedicated the rest of his life pouring into the lives of young Black men. He states that his goal is to help these young men learn to be responsible and an example of what a man should be. Mr. Lott is free internally and externally. Despite his circumstances and even through them, he was able to find purpose and meaning. His life is impacting the lives of so many others.

## Reflect:

As Kierkegaard stated, life must be lived forward but can only be understood looking backward. Thinking back, are there places in your life where you could not see the impact of your story on the life of another person until it was over? How would you describe that situation?

_____

_____

_____

_____

_____

_____

It has been said that the opposite of faith is not doubt; it is control. Is there any place in your story where you are seeking to control your impact? Where do you need to surrender control and trust God's vision for impact in your life?

_____

_____

_____

_____

_____

_____

Hope is the greatest antidote to despair. Where are you still waiting for God to demonstrate impact? Is it in a relationship or a situation? List those here and ask God to work according to his will in those situations.

_____

_____

_____

_____

_____

_____

Where do you need God's help to see your circumstances as God sees them?

_____

_____

_____

_____

_____

_____

_____

# CHAPTER 8

# THE PURPOSES OF JESUS

"The thief comes only to steal and kill and destroy; <u>I have come that you might have life,</u> and have it to the full" (John 10:10, emphasis added). This is the declared purpose of Jesus. He taught in contrast to our enemy that He was here so that we might discover abundant life. He was not just talking about some future eternal reality in the clouds. Rather, he was talking about giving people real physical, emotional, and spiritual wellness that sets the world ablaze.

When Jesus makes his bold declaration, He is expressing His purpose to bring not only eternal life but also a life of fullness, meaning, and joy in the here and now. This statement contrasts with the "thief" who seeks to "steal, kill, and destroy" Jesus stands confident in his own ability to fulfill his promise. Offering instead a vision of life that is rich in purpose, peace, and connection with God.

To live "abundantly" in Jesus' terms means more than just material prosperity or ease; it refers to a spiritual wholeness—a life marked by love, joy, peace, and purpose. Jesus offers a path to reconcile with God, freeing people from sin and opening the way to a life empowered by God's love and guidance. This abundant life includes:

1. **Spiritual Fulfillment**: Jesus invites us to a relationship with God, which brings deep spiritual satisfaction, even amid life's challenges.

2. **Purpose and Calling**: An abundant life aligns with God's purpose for us, allowing us to use our gifts in ways that bless others and contribute to God's kingdom.

3. **Inner Peace and Joy**: Through Jesus, we receive peace that surpasses circumstances and joy rooted in God's promises and faithfulness.

4. **Relational Wholeness**: Living abundantly also means healing and enriching our relationships, as Jesus' teachings guide us in love, forgiveness, and compassion.

In essence, Jesus' promise of abundant life is about living with a depth of purpose, connection, and fulfillment that transcends mere existence, inviting us into a life that reflects the fullness of God's love and His intentions for us.

In 1 Peter 3:15, Peter admonishes us to always be ready to give an answer for the hope that we have in Christ. That is, when we are following Christ, fully alive, just as He has declared we would be, that kind of hope will leak out and cause others to question us. Jesus came to ensure that we flourish and live the kind of life that causes other people to wonder and inquire about this strange peace, hope, and joy and love. He came so that we might have a meaningful human experience that connects Earth to the eternal kingdom. We are the fulfillment of the Lord's prayer for God's kingdom to come on earth as it is in Heaven.

With this broad declaration in mind, it would be easy to ask, "Don't all Christians have the same purpose?" However, this oversimplification dismisses the reality that God's achievement of this life happens through a complex tapestry of human diversity. Breadth of connection does not diminish the personal nature of God's design and unique assignment for each of us. We are unified in purpose, but we are not uniform in expression. Our purpose will be a unique expression of God's plan for humanity. His plan for humanity is more complex than we could dream. Our purpose won't contradict the purposes of Jesus, but as individuals, none of us are the full expression of His ultimate plan. Collectively, we are a display for His glory and the fulfillment of His declaration.

I did not realize that I had literally co-opted the purpose of Jesus when I discovered that God was drawing my purpose from Isaiah 61. In fact, I was wrapping up my first attempt at extended fasting when I learned that Jesus had declared Himself to be the fulfillment of Isaiah Chapter 61 at the end of His time in the wilderness. In Luke chapter 4, we read that Jesus was led by the Holy Spirit into the wilderness to be tempted by Satan for 40 days. During that time, He engaged in an extended fast. My eyes nearly popped out of my head when I realized the similarity and significance. When He emerged, he went to Nazareth and read the Isaiah 61 scroll to the Jews in the synagogue, declaring that He is the fulfillment of that prophecy and then He sat down. The devoutly religious people are furious because this is a public admission that Jesus is the Messiah. He was stepping into his identity publicly. Nearly everyone listening would have heard this as blasphemy, a crime punishable by death. The crowd tries to seize Him, but the scripture says that He walked right through the crowd and went on His way. It wasn't His time to die. Jesus declared his purpose and set off a riot.

The same could be true for us. If we are to really connect our life purpose to Jesus, it will ignite something. The supernatural fire that burns inside of someone who is living out the purpose for which he or she is designed casts a unique light. People will be drawn to the flame. As John Mark Comer states, we have to not just ask ourselves, what would Jesus do, but what would Jesus do if he was living the life that I am living.

If you are still unsure what your purpose is, you can borrow the purpose of Jesus. He stated His purpose like this, "I have come that you might have life and have it to the full." In the message, it is termed, "that they may have real and eternal life, more and better life than they ever dreamed of." In John 14, he declares that He Himself is life. This means that as we authentically pursue Jesus, we are pursuing purpose and life. Our divine purpose connects to the purpose of Jesus. He wants us to find our purpose and learn to live it.

There are five primary activities that Jesus says He is on earth to fulfill:

1. Preach the gospel–the Kingdom of God is near (there is a new way available).

2. Proclaim freedom– You don't have to be in bondage.

3. Remove oppression

4. Bring sight to people—help people see

5. Proclaim God's favor on people– God already loves you.

All of us, as we live out our unique purpose, will connect with the activities of Jesus. It's important to remember that the sacred vs. secular divide is something that we created in response to modern America. We know in the Great Commission in Matthew 28 that each believer is charged to make disciples. However, we don't see Him walking around telling people that they need to go into the ministry, leaving their vocation.

In the original language, the word here for "go" could be translated as a present participle or a progressive verb tense. In other words, the best bible translations will communicate this verse as continuous motion or "As you are Going, make disciples." "As you are going" includes the real life we are living right now. Our purpose is not something we must go off and find; rather it is found as we are pursuing the life that God has given to us. Jesus' purpose is ours to borrow and our responsibility to steward in the relationships and circles of influence in which we move. The purposes of Jesus are not spiritual platitudes; rather the principles work themselves out in very human, real ways.

We are to preach the gospel or to make it known that the message of Jesus is good news. In practical terms, this means we are encouraging and diligent in the work that we do. We are to proclaim freedom with our lives. Functionally, we don't live in bondage. We consistently submit our lives to Jesus and allow Him to break off addictions and attitudes that don't permit freedom inside of us. We confront our sin so that it doesn't easily entangle us and make us unfruitful.

We remove oppression. Pragmatically, this looks like keeping our eyes open to systems of abuse. It means paying attention to our own tendencies toward power hoarding. Seeking the benefit of others even when they are not in the room. We are to bring sight to people or help them see. This means that we are truth-tellers to ourselves and others. I do not mean that we walk around being brutally candid with people, but rather that we are gentle and honest. We resist the urge to engage in conspiracy and gossip. We are dedicated to being clear-minded and discrete in communication. We are to proclaim God's favor to those around us.

God is more gracious than we could ever hope to be with humanity. In a world where people are dying from hopelessness, we need to be messengers of hope, declaring the good news that Jesus loves people. He is not standing in Heaven, arms crossed, angrily waiting for us to change. He came to earth, and we are in His good graces. Romans 2:4 tells us that God's kindness, his patience with us, is an invitational mechanism drawing us to repent. Unfortunately, Christians are known to declare judgment instead of favor. Perhaps if we join with Jesus in His approach, we will see the repentance that we know is needed for salvation. Jesus was <u>dedicated</u> to the mission of His life, which was to preach the good news of the kingdom of God...in His words, "because this is why I was sent." Likewise, we have been sent by Him to do the same. With all of the above stated, it would still be easy for me to fall into the uniform-Christian-purpose camp, deeming unique purpose humanly impossible, if it weren't for Jesus' parting words in the 14th chapter of John. In preparing to leave, Jesus was assuring His disciples that His imminent death, which they did not yet understand, was necessary. He says that He must go away so that "The Helper" can come. He goes on in John 14:12, making one of his boldest statements, "anyone who has faith in me will do what I have been doing. He will do *even greater things than these*, because I am going to the Father." Greater things, Jesus? Greater things. This idea is coming from the man who never sinned, who raised the dead, healed the sick, cured the blind, overthrew corrupt religious activity, welcomed women and children in a society where they held very little value, and crossed racial boundaries. Greater things? That seems like a tall order. And it would be, if not for the Holy Spirit. Jesus left with us the Comforter, the Helper, God, the Holy Spirit.

What is crazy to me about His declaration is that we are the multiplied impact of Jesus. If we are living our lives on purpose and connecting with the purposes of Jesus in our daily pursuits, we are His purpose mechanism at scale. Because He lives inside of us, it is truly possible that we will do greater things. Individually and collectively, we will be the expression of Jesus' vision that His kingdom can manifest on the earth. While it still boggles my mind, we have this promise that He can do more than we can imagine. My personal comprehension of how He works is not required for it to be happening. He operates outside of reason and human imagination. Greater things we will do in our circles of influence, with our talents, living out our dreams, healing from our disappointments, so that we may help others heal.

Find your unique purpose and learn to live it. Own your design and hone your talents, wake up your desires and dreams. Live your life on purpose and watch the full life of Jesus impact those around you.

## Reflect:

How do you see Jesus show up in your life?

_____

_____

_____

_____

_____

_____

_____

Which one of the activities of Jesus most resonates with you? Why do you think that is?

_____

_____

_____

_____

_____

_____

What are the practical ways that you can connect your purpose to the purposes of Jesus?

_____

_____

_____

_____

_____

_____

## Prayer:

Open the eyes of my heart, Lord. I know that any time we pray in alignment with Your will we can be confident that it will happen. It is Your will that people encounter You through the healthy expression of me fully alive with Your Spirit. Help me to see the ways You have already given me the opportunity to bring Your purposes to those around me. Help me to have faith that You really have 'greater things' for me to do in Your power.

## CHAPTER 9

# CONTENDING FOR YOUR PURPOSE

"It is not the critic who counts; not the man who points out how the strong man stumbles or where the doer of deeds could have done them better. The credit belongs to the man who is actually in the arena, whose face is marred by dust and sweat and blood; who strives valiantly; who errs, and comes short again and again, because there is no effort without error and shortcoming; but who does actually strive to do the deeds; who knows the great enthusiasms, the great devotions; who spends himself in a worthy cause; who at the best knows in the end the triumph of high achievement, and who at the worst, if he fails, at least fails while daring greatly, so that his place shall never be with those cold and timid souls who know neither victory nor defeat."
—Theodore Roosevelt

The thing about purpose is it's worth fighting for. It is work to find it and it is work to keep living in it. Once we recognize the magnitude of living in our purpose, that kind of vigor nearly invites opposition because our purpose plays a role in human redemption. For each of us, our purpose is our unique effort to make the world right; to create the world as it should be. It is the answer to the prayer that Jesus taught us to pray, "Lord, your kingdom come, your will be done, on earth as it is in heaven" (Matthew 6:10). Each time we move toward our purpose, we are echoing that prayer. Sometimes because of the familiarity of those phrases, we can miss the significance. When we bring God's kingdom to Earth by living out our purpose, that movement has an eternal impact. We push back the darkness that seeks to set itself up against God's kingdom. When we walk in step with our purpose, we bring Heaven to Earth in our spheres of influence. When we each live like that, it is a glimpse of what is to come. It is a mysterious mingling of Heaven and Earth, fleshly but strangely spiritual.

Our purpose is the gift God gives to us. Living our purpose is the offering we give back to Him. With this in mind, it makes sense that when we live out our purpose, we will experience opposition. If our purpose was merely human rather than God-given, then it might not be worthy of opposition. However, if our purpose is otherworldly, a means for pushing back darkness, it stands to reason that our purpose would be opposed. In Ephesians, we read an admonition to remember that our battle as followers of Jesus is almost never man-to-man. Rather, we are pushing against forces that, while unseen, are very real and present. Ephesians 6:12 (HCSB) states, "For our battle is not against flesh and blood, but against the rulers, against the authorities, against the world power of this darkness, against the spiritual forces of evil in the heavens." In this note, Paul is reminding the believers that while we may experience fleshly opposition, we must look past what our eyes see to notice the forces that drive our fight.

There are three blind spots that believers can have when it comes to contending for their purpose. The first is that we don't recognize that there is a battle at all, the second is we mistake our enemy, and the third is that we fear the battle itself and choose to remain on the sidelines. The consequences of each of these blind spots are different, but the impact is similar. When we don't fight or when we fight the wrong opponent, our purpose may not materialize. Plainly, our potential and our lived experience will be stifled. The place in which we were destined to make the world right with our light remains dimmed.

When we don't recognize that there is a battle that we are meant to fight, our experience of trials and hardship can take on an interpretive lens. Specifically, we can take the struggle to mean that maybe we are not on the right path. Perhaps this sense of motivation that I have toward this idea or need was not really God's leading. If we don't understand that the battle is evidence of our purpose rather than an indicator that we are off course, it is easy for our unique contribution to be thwarted. In response to the suffering, a common response is to seek comfort and ease. Don't get me wrong, I don't mean this to sound like we should go running after a struggle; rather, that when struggle comes (and it will), we respond to it with a knowing anticipation. We should not be surprised that living our purpose invites resistance. When we have battle awareness, the bullets coming our way are a reminder to fight rather than retreat. It is easy to take someone out in a battle they didn't expect.

The second blind spot is when we mistake our enemy. This is probably the most common blind spot, but we must persevere toward our purpose. Notice that in the Ephesians 6 passage, Paul is describing our enemy through contrast. He is saying our enemy is this, not that. If this was not a common pitfall, he would not have utilized so many descriptions of the battle forces. Paul states our battle is NOT against flesh and blood. He is encouraging us to consider another dimension of reality. In most of our lived experiences, our battle feels like it is against flesh and blood. If we consider only what we can see, taste, smell, feel, and hear, we would be right. When we are young, it feels like our battle is against our siblings and parents. They are who we can see. In middle school, it seems like our fight is against the mean girls. They are who we can hear. As we get older, it seems like we are struggling against our boss or our spouse. They are the ones that seem responsible for at least half of our experiences.

Paul is calling us to look past mere appearances. He is saying yes, there is a flesh and blood component to the struggle. However, that is not the real force behind the fight. *People* are never the real enemy. The real power you are facing is dark, spiritual, and evil. If we do not recognize who we are fighting and we mistake our enemy to be our spouse or neighbor, we cease being in the battle against our true enemy and instead become his soldiers. In other words, we become agents of human destruction rather than ambassadors of redemption. When we mistake our enemy, the battle becomes a one-sided victory with redemption as the loser.

I don't mean to sound dramatic, but your purpose is literally that important. When you live it out, you are pushing back darkness in your workplace, in your family, in your neighborhood. The power we walk in is spiritual power. If we fail to see that the people in front of us, though it may seem that they are against us, are only being *used* by our true enemy, it changes our warrior stance.

Some individuals find themselves prey to the third blind spot. They recognize that there is a battle, that it is not a human battle, and that we have a real enemy. However, the very recognition of this dimension causes them to say "no thank you" to living out their purpose. They recognize that there is real risk and danger involved in pushing back darkness and living our purpose. That risk is more than they are interested in taking. They may say things like, "I'm not strong like you," or "God has enough people serving in that capacity. He doesn't really need me." There may even be lazy theology involved around the belief that God's purposes always prevail regardless of personal behavior. This sideline-stander has just enough warmth from the fire of the fight that they are not motivated to act, but they are missing the fact that abdication is not a neutral response. Not only are they missing out on the spark of life but the people in their spheres of influence are also living in the shadows that will not be illuminated. Perhaps this darkness will not have a salvific impact, but it definitely has a battle impact. Someone needed you fighting by their side. Someone needed your light to eradicate the last corner of evil in their world, but you left them in the dark. Scared. Alone. Searching. Not only do we leave that interpersonal impact, we cheat ourselves of the strength that comes from battle.

The battle produces things that peace simply can't. We see in James chapter 1 that as we persevere through suffering, we gain a <u>completing</u> gift. James 1:2-4 states, "Consider it a great joy, my brothers, whenever you experience various trials, knowing that the testing of your faith produces endurance. But endurance must do its complete work, so that you may be mature and complete, lacking nothing" (HCSB). In this passage, we see that as we endure hardship—testing trials—we have a chance to see it for what it is. Difficult battles are formative. When we submit to God's plan for that battle, knowing that He is using the enemy's efforts against him and for us, it changes our posture toward the battle, making way for the finished work.

Battles are a vehicle for maturity and completion. Another translation talks about "persevering" under trial. The root idea from the Greek is that we "stay under" the trial so that the trial can deliver or complete its intended outcome—maturity. If we look closely in this passage we see the importance of our *mindset* toward the battle. The call to consider it joy is a mindset call. We must intentionally view the battle as an opportunity to gain strength. James is not flatly dismissing the difficulty, asking us to adopt toxic positivity toward the trials we face. Rather, he says, look past the trial to see what is offered on the other side. Change your mindset toward trial because if you understand the role that the battle plays, it will change how you experience it.

Just as we have to look past the enemy in front of us to recognize the forces we face, we can also learn to see those very forces of darkness as the catalyst to our maturity. This is also known as developing resilience. Resilient people bounce back from hardship stronger than they were before the hardship. A fun fact about resilience is that it cannot be developed through comfort and ease. While rest is certainly critical to developing resilience, it needs to be an active recovery response to something difficult or draining in order for it to be resilient. The kind of laughable reality that believers get to embrace as we learn to endure the battle with joy is that the very thing that is aiming to debilitate or deplete us is the same experience that will give us the overcoming, maturity and complete strength we need to live our purpose fully. In nature, we see this principle of struggle producing strength as we study the phases of metamorphosis. According to the Oxford Dictionary, "metamorphosis is the process of transformation from an immature form to an adult form in two or more distinct stages." One of the most common ways to teach children metamorphosis is to study the stages of a butterfly. The butterfly changes through four distinct stages: egg, larva (caterpillar), chrysalis, and adult. What we may not remember from elementary school, however, is the necessity of struggle that is involved in this process of change. In order for the butterfly to fully emerge as an adult, he must break free from the chrysalis through pushing, tearing, and fighting. If a well-meaning bystander were to "help" the butterfly escape by tearing or cutting the walls of the chrysalis, the action would inhibit the butterfly from developing the strength he needs as an adult. He would fail to fly because the strength needed to flap his wings is developed through the struggle of escape. That is to say, the fight to get out was necessary to his development. He could not fully function as a butterfly if that battle did not exist.

The same is true for us; we must persevere through the fight, understanding that the battle is necessary to develop the strength it will take for us to live out our given purpose. As we struggle and fight and endure through trials, humility and confidence emerge. We are refined by the battle in ways that comfort will not deliver. Our character is made complete in the struggle. These trials are making us battle-ready with the strength we need to contend for our purpose.

I consider my purpose in life to be: "To bind up the brokenhearted and set the captives free." I suppose you can't have a purpose statement like mine and escape suffering. You can't bind up broken hearts having never endured a broken heart. You can't set captives free if you have not experienced significant levels of bondage. I simply wouldn't be equipped to live this purpose without battling through the thing I was called to do.

When I was a junior in college, after battling some of the deepest valleys of depression I had ever seen, I felt like the Lord made it clear to me that my purpose on the planet was going to be about strengthening the hearts of others who have had their hearts broken too. I did a Bible study by Beth Moore called "Breaking Free," and the whole study is based on Isaiah 61, which says,

> "The Spirit of the Sovereign LORD is on me,
> because the LORD has anointed me
> to proclaim good news to the poor.
> He has sent me to **bind up the brokenhearted,**
> **to proclaim freedom for the captives**
> and release from darkness for the prisoners,[a]
>
> to proclaim the year of the LORD's favor
> and the day of vengeance of our God,
> to comfort all who mourn,
>
> and provide for those who grieve in Zion—
> to bestow on them a crown of beauty
> instead of ashes,
> the oil of joy
> instead of mourning,
> and a garment of praise
> instead of a spirit of despair."
> They will be called oaks of righteousness,
> a planting of the LORD
> for the display of his splendor."
> –Isaiah 61:1-3 (emphasis added)

There it was....like it hopped off the page. "Bind up the brokenhearted and set the captives free." The words burned in my heart. I remembered vividly at the time feeling so hopeless, so broken. It was a feeling that my twenty-something self didn't expect to happen post-salvation. Was I supposed to have the God of all peace and comfort living inside of me and feel like dying? I had to wrestle with that. The truth was, if I didn't get my heart broken, I'm not sure I would have had the same experience with His healing mercies. Without the breaking, the binding up would not have come. Jesus had bound up my broken heart and I knew that the healing I had received was now mine to dispense. Mysteriously, the calling of Jesus to bind up brokenness had become mine too. Somehow, this healing gave birth to purpose in my heart. Beauty from ashes.

It would have made sense to me for that single instance of despair and healing to be sufficient experience with brokenness to propel my whole life. Not everyone who contends with depression lives to tell the story, yet I had. However, single battle purpose is not the way purpose works. When God gives us the grace to see our divine purpose, it will be tested again and again. Purpose, much like the rooting of an oak tree, must endure testing to be found true. Just as robust winds propel growth and deepening for the root system of a tree, the testing of our faith roots our purpose and produces determination in us. It is not that God has lost faith in us or that we have lost our purpose; it is that purpose must be tested in order for it to grow in genuineness. We contend many battles so that we can be taken to full maturity.

One of the greatest barriers to maturing in our purpose is our ability to discern ideologies and presumptions that impact the world around us. There are cultural ideologies that set themselves up as barriers to finding and fulfilling our purpose. In 2 Corinthians 10:5, Paul talks about the lofty ideas that set themselves up against the knowledge of Christ. He says that "we demolish arguments and every pretense that sets itself up against the knowledge of God." One such pretense that I see setting itself up today is just the ideology or belief around the goodness of work. There is a growing dissatisfaction that presents itself in conversations about work. The prevailing idea is that work is an inconvenience to life. That work sucks and it always will. It is something to bear or, better yet, something to escape. This ideology currently presents itself as a funny meme or a silly social media video mocking work. There is a "lazy girlfriend" or "house husband" mentality that is being lifted up as a desirable way to spend time. This idea communicates that the goal of life is to do as little as possible for the most amount of money.

However, I believe this ideology is a pretense against the healthy pursuit of purpose. Our work, whether paid or unpaid, is often the very way we begin to experience a sense of purpose and contribution to humanity. Rather than work being an inconvenience, it can be meaningful. We all have something meaningful to contribute. As long as people try to escape doing work, they won't be able to find the sense of purpose they so desperately need to find.

I was recently talking with a friend who is in between work opportunities. He has plenty of skills and is genuinely a hard-working person who wants to make the world a better place. He and his partner have enough income and physical provisions to live a good life. However, he finds himself looking for something meaningful to do. He said, "I don't mind doing the househusband things. But the general feelings of aimlessness are getting old." He knows inherently that doing nothing or even doing whatever he wants all day eventually gets old. He wants to work because he finds meaning and purpose in that pursuit. It is the same for each of us. It is important that we find or create healthy workplaces. However, escaping from work altogether should not be the goal. Work was not the curse in the garden. We were created with a contributory desire. We have been convinced that work is an inconvenience. It's an ideological trap that sets the next generation up for languishing and purposelessness.

Our purpose is a gift. Work is a gift. The ability to meaningfully contribute is a gift and as we fight for it, we will face discouragement. We must ask ourselves, what am I going to believe about myself, about my role in this world, about God, and about others? We have to identify the ideologies we may have adopted that are in opposition to our purpose. It is understandable and even common for discouragement in purpose to trigger a desire to isolate or withdraw. Isolation, however, is the kill shot to purpose. Since purpose is a gift that we use to benefit others, when we isolate ourselves from those we are called to serve, the pilot light of purpose is extinguished. This is why we must fight to stay in the game. We must maintain the inner fire that purpose brings.

Finally, it is important to know that we don't have to fight alone. It is tempting in Western Christianity to view the Christian life as Me+Jesus. However, we were not meant to walk alone. While a relationship with Jesus is very personal, it is not private. The maxim, "Don't talk about religion or politics at the dinner table," has crept into Christian practice to make us more isolated than we should be. First-century Christianity assumed a faith community was involved. It assumes that as you pursue your purpose there will be a group of people around you to strengthen, advise, and encourage you in your journey. The Christian life is both yours and ours. It is both personal and corporate. We see in the book of Acts that the early church met daily in one another's homes (Acts 2:46). It would be very hard to pretend around church friends who saw you every day. It would be harder to hide our sadness, questions, and fears. I believe this type of spiritual community was much better suited to help each other face discouragement. If we are going to stay in the fight, we have to let some people get close enough to fight with us. We need an army to march into this battle.

Jesus guaranteed that we would have trouble, and we are to strengthen one another. We can overcome many things in prayer for one another that we cannot overcome by ourselves.

In Matthew 18:20, Jesus promises to be with us when we gather in His name. A single warrior standing alone can be defeated, but an army of believers agreeing together for God's purpose will not be overcome. We need to be reminded of who God is and of who we are. We can borrow the faith of our community as our own faith falters.

## Reflect:

Do you find yourself in the middle of a fight for your purpose? Are you discouraged? What do you need right now?

_____

_____

_____

_____

_____

_____

_____

Are there any lies you need to fight with the truth?

_____

_____

_____

_____

_____

_____

_____

Do you feel like you may be operating with a blind spot to the battle for your purpose? Which one? What impact is that having?

Who are you going to war with?

_____

_____

_____

_____

_____

_____

_____

_____

_____

## Prayer:

Lord, I know You have created me with purpose. I am getting weary in the fight and need You to renew me. Thank You for being my strength in the middle of weakness. Please illuminate my blind spots with Your truth. Help me to fight with perseverance toward Your kingdom coming on earth.

# CHAPTER 10
# PURSUING PURPOSE

**"Wisdom is distilled thinking from the throne room."**
**—Graham Cooke**

I think Mary Oliver asked it best when she said, "Tell me, what is it you plan to do with your one wild and precious life?" This is the question each of us must grapple with. As much as we would like to deny our mortality, each of us will die. According to psychologist Erik Erikson, everyone goes through a developmental ladder where we grapple with various conflict points. As we age, these conflicts turn toward the meaning of life. Between the ages of 65 and death, we begin to ask ourselves, did I live a meaningful life? Did I accomplish what I should have? Reflectively, as we age, we will begin to ask ourselves, what did I do with the life I lived? Am I proud or disappointed? The challenge is, if we wait until our life is over to ask that question, there is very little to be done about the answer. However, if we ask ourselves these questions and intentionally pursue a purposeful answer, we are more likely to affirmatively reflect about the life that we live. Purpose is the gift that keeps giving. It benefits us in discovery, pursuit, in trial, and in reflection.

It is paramount to you and to those who love you most that you are diligent in finding and living your purpose. By now, I hope you are reflecting through the questions at the end of the sections and finding ways to articulate your own sense of purpose. It is likely you need to dialogue out some of the aspects of your own purpose formula. Many people get sidelined by the disappointments of life that feel like an interruption of purpose. I hope that section of the book encourages you to think about how those circumstances might, in fact, be something of a golden repair for you. Ask God to think with you about those past circumstances or talk through it with a trusted spiritual advisor, wise friend, or counselor. The goal of this book is to give you guideposts to identify and live out your purpose. I'm going to tell a few stories of real people who have discovered and are living out their purpose to help you imagine your own journey to living free, full of purpose. The steps are below:

1. Identify your purpose formula
2. Focus on pathways in front of you
3. Get God's perspective on current circumstances
4. Trust God with the vision for impact
5. Connect with the purpose of Jesus
6. Find your army
7. Contend for your purpose

Finally, I want to encourage you. It is so easy to lose sight of our purpose because the difficulties of life can be so discouraging. It is hard to find a sense of peace with our purpose when we feel like we are in the middle of a storm. One phrase that I have repeated to myself over and over as I'm seeking to be faithful in living my purpose is "rest, not quit." When I'm failing to see progress or worse, things seem to be declining in the face of my efforts to make a difference; it is tempting to run away or to quit. This experience usually hits me as a sensation like I want to burn it all down. Meaning, I want to destroy the very things I have been working to see happen. I have learned to feel that sensation and interpret it as a time to take a break to rest. Once I rest, that is the point at which I begin to reflect on my current state to determine what needs to change or shift. Sometimes, resting is enough. When I'm rested, my perspective is often renewed. As my dad told me when I was a teenager, sometimes the most spiritual thing we can do is take a nap.

Resting or Sabbath has become kind of a trendy topic in Christian circles because our tech-saturated world and over-scheduled lives are draining us. Rest is a tool to combat a constant sense of movement and productivity that is always in front of us. The importance of rest in pursuit of purpose cannot be overstated. One of the temptations of pursuing purpose, once we find it, is to constantly contribute. There are endless opportunities to say yes to things that could be purposeful for us, or that could benefit from our involvement. However, if we are constantly depleted because of our pursuits, it eventually leads to burnout. While purpose is a burnout buffer, if we get stuck in overdrive, our physical and emotional tanks will run low. As Vince Lombardi famously said, "Fatigue makes cowards of us all." Exhaustion can eat away at the courage needed to make our highest contribution. Being worn out and battered is not evidence that we are being faithful with our purpose. It is more likely an indicator that we might not make it to the finish line.

There is a model in Scripture for being mightily used by God and then immediately succumbing to the beast of exhaustion. In 1 Kings 19, we see Elijah having just defeated an entire nation of the prophets of Baal. He was the instrument God used to show power and shame the pagan diviners. Elijah had just called down fire from Heaven that fully consumed a wet altar sacrifice in a truly miraculous display of divine power. He was then able to massacre the prophets in a total defeat of dark power.

What happens next in the story is such a clear display of the threat of fatigue. God had used Elijah to demonstrate his power in a way that left no questions that he was God's man. This is a testament that Elijah was walking in God-ordained purpose. Yet, doubt crept in. The day after he has had the most unparalleled experience working as God's prophet, we see Elijah trembling in fear because Jezebel, the king's wife, is threatening his life. When King Ahab shared the news of the prophets' total defeat with Jezebel, the queen, she was enraged and issued a threat on Elijah's life. Mind you, Elijah was just a party to God's miraculous delivery.

> "Then Jezebel sent a messenger to Elijah, saying, "So may the gods do to me, and more also, if I do not make your life like the life of one of them by this time tomorrow." Then he was afraid; he got up and fled for his life, and came to Beer-sheba, which belongs to Judah; he left his servant there."
>
> 1 Kings 19:2-3, ESV

Jezebel is invoking the power of the gods that the prophets had been unable to summon. However, because of his level of weariness, he did not show up with the same level of confidence for deliverance despite his experiences with God. We see Elijah respond to this threat by running away and despairing of his own life. Chapter 19 goes on to say:

> "But [Elijah] went on a day's journey into the wilderness and came and sat down under a broom tree. And he asked

that he might die, saying, 'It is enough; now, O LORD, take away my life, for I am no better than my fathers.'"

1 Kings 19:4, ESV

Do you see that? Elijah, a mighty prophet of God, feels insignificant and crushed. Have you ever felt that way? I have. It is easy to think that we have been off in our calling or that our life maybe doesn't mean what we hoped it did. It is significant to me how God chose to meet Elijah's needs. He did not admonish Elijah for his attitude or lack of faith. Instead, He sent an angel to minister to meet Elijah's physical needs.

"And he [Elijah] lay down and slept under a broom tree. And behold, an angel touched him and said to him, "Arise and eat." And he looked, and behold, there was at his head a cake baked on hot stones and a jar of water. And he ate and drank and lay down again. And the angel of the LORD came again a second time and touched him and said, "Arise and eat, for the journey is too great for you." And he arose and ate and drank, and went in the strength of that food forty days and forty nights to Horeb, the mount of God."

1 Kings 19:5-8, ESV

We see that God moved to meet Elijah's physical needs, and from that, he gained spiritual vigor again. It is the same with us. Sometimes we overthink. We may question our purpose or circumstances. We may question ourselves, or like Elijah, the very point of our lives. However, what God might use to meet our needs is a good nap and a nourishing meal.

He would want to die at the hands of the same God who had just mightily shown others the nearness of Elijah to true power. "The biggest battlefield that we face is the mind," Pastor Bill Johnson says. We saw Elijah succeed in his purpose in an actual battle of prophets. However, we see him struggle even more dramatically in the battle of his mind. How often is this our experience too?

However, God, in infinite wisdom, rather than granting Elijah's requested end, sends an angel to feed him and tell him to take a nap. Discouragement in purpose is normal. We need to teach ourselves to rest in the face of discouragement. When we burn out, we must learn to renew our strength in normal, natural ways as well as spiritual, supernatural ways. Rest and recovery are critical to living out our purpose and persisting. One of the ways I help myself recover is by reviewing what is true. Although this quote was written several thousand years after he lived, I like to believe that it would have brought Elijah some of the same relief it has brought me through the years as I have learned to recover and rise to keep fighting.

The goal of our lives, fully poured out, is a long obedience in the same direction. We should view it as a life-long contribution of service to the world where we are walking with Jesus, hearing His voice saying, *This is the way, walk in it. Here is the stream and the still water, lie down a while on the journey and rest. Come to Me if you are weary, I will give you rest.* These admonitions to rest and to walk presume that we are both intentionally living the highest contribution of our lives and that we are doing so in a way that incorporates healthy rhythms of rest.

# CHAPTER 11

# WALKING IN PURPOSE

"I got a greater purpose. God put something in my heart to get across and that's what I'm going to focus on, using my voice as an instrument and doing what needs to be done."
—Kendrick Lamar

## Hannah Schmidt

It can be tempting to believe that you have to have it all figured out before you can have an impact in the lives of others. Hannah Schmidt is living proof that you can live out your purpose from the messy middle. She would describe herself as still figuring out what her purpose is. She is mother to three small kids, wife to Brian, and recently sold her first start-up business. If you press her, Hannah would tell you that her purpose is to have unlikely conversations that leave people feeling valued... to tell stories that communicate the unique value and worth of each person. In the next breath, she would also tell you that she finds the whole conversation about purpose to be a bit cloudy. There have always been voices pressing into her sense of direction, telling her that her vision and purpose needs to be specifically vocational.

As a young girl, Hannah always had a strong sense of drive and desire to work. She started working at church, then babysitting. Next, she worked at a bowling alley and then in retail spaces at age 15. If there was work to be done, she signed herself up to contribute and earn money. In her own memory of growing up, she was "overworked and overscheduled." When she got married and moved to Oklahoma City with her husband for his job, she found herself without a job for the first time since she was a teenager. This felt significant. "Who am I if I'm not working?" She said, "Busyness is a way the enemy has always distracted me." When she was without work for four months, this was the first time since she was eligible to work that she was not doing so. That space gave her time to reflect on what she really wanted to be doing with her gifts and talents.

In college, Hannah studied Journalism. That major positioned her to have conversations with people with whom she would not normally cross paths. "I was given a job where it was ok to be curious and to make people feel seen and heard and make them want to talk to you." Her natural interest in others and that educational experience sparked a desire to dig deeper into the stories of others. Hannah has a knack for putting others at ease. Those who know her well would describe her as a good listener, authentic, and real. Her optimism and empathic awareness naturally position her to be someone with whom people feel safe. Couple these gifts with her joyful countenance, and she is well positioned to see the real person behind any situation. Hannah believes the best in people, and her ability to communicate the value she sees in others creates space for people to see their own value.

After a difficult miscarriage and a deep desire to be a mom was held in question, some of the professional drive was right-sized. Along with a few professional experiences that treated working motherhood as a gauntlet to be run, Hannah knew that she needed to find a different work-life integration strategy. Strict work from home proved to be a challenge with young kids underfoot. She began to look for a co-working space that would provide the necessary separation between work and home. As she searched other co-working spaces, the vibe was off. The culture of many co-working spaces catered to men. While Hannah is explicitly pro-human (not just pro-woman), she felt the need to find a space that catered more to the needs of women in the workforce. She wanted to find a place where women could build strong interpersonal relationships and support one another in their successes.

Sometimes, building what you personally need is the provision others are praying to find. As her search for the right co-working space returned void, it became clear to Hannah that she needed to build her own co-working space tailored to female entrepreneurs. Lots of people had opinions on how she should do this. Several commercial real-estate owners discouraged the idea, explicitly stating the likelihood that a women-only co-working space could be a successful business model was very slim. Yet, Hannah persisted in her vision to build a space where women could be seen and uplifted. She used her drive to know people and to build an authentic community of women supporting women as a rallying cry to find the right kind members for her new business. She named her venture "The Treasury," and her members were called "Treasures." Even the nomenclature communicated the desire to communicate value to others. Each detail of her business emanated her desire to cultivate unlikely conversations that communicate worthiness.

In the earliest start-up phase for The Treasury, Hannah received advice to position herself as the expert entrepreneur as a means of attracting members. However, that positioning felt inauthentic to Hannah's natural wiring. Instead, she had a strong desire to facilitate conversations rather than lead as an expert. As she began to run the business, Hannah quickly realized that there were things she needed to learn about being an entrepreneur. In response to that need, she would invite speakers to have open conversations on the topics that new entrepreneurs needed to learn. She says, "We had these couch chats early on…which were literally just an opportunity for me to ask questions. I would invite other people so it wasn't weird. So I would do a Q&A on topics I needed to know." These conversations turned into valuable member benefits for the Treasures. In following her own instincts, she found another way to draw people in and live out her purpose. "People are not attracted to you for what you know… it is for truly seeing them. It is such a freeing realization that you don't have to have it all together to influence people. You can consistently tell people you have no idea what you are doing."

As she lived out her purpose authentically, Hannah began to see others respond. "People are going to be watching you because…you are taking up your God-given space and nothing else. And I really thought at the beginning I was going to have to be everything." People began asking questions about how she was freeing herself from limiting beliefs like the need to be constantly available as a business owner. In her most recent maternity leave, she did not leave people a way to call her so she could stay tuned into her own season. This simple but purposeful decision communicated that Hannah was going to create her own way as a mother, as a community builder, and as a business owner. In living out her purpose and rightly ordering her priorities, Hannah was breathing life and permission to do the same into her community of women.

Hannah recently sold that business to a new owner who is profoundly impacted by the work Hannah began. Even in her handoff of that project, Hannah allowed another woman to live out a dream she had for stewarding the kind of female community co-working space that Hannah had envisioned and built. As for Hannah, she is onto her next purpose project. Selling the business gave her space to fully focus on another project she had envisioned which communicates the unique value and worth of women.

Hannah is currently in the process of publishing the third issue of the Hundred Magazine. "The Hundred," as it is known, is a magazine dedicated to telling the stories of "Wildly capable women making a difference in Oklahoma City." The distinct feature of this magazine is that the stories feature the character of women making a difference rather than women who are making purely professional achievements. She states, "When I pick up a list of 'powerful' or 'top' women today, I see pages of women celebrated for their title and influence. Perhaps the publishers want us to feel like if we try hard enough, someday we, too, can be bank executives or married to wealthy men. But when my daughter picks up a list of 'top' women someday, I want it to be ones with true character, not just title. I want them to have names she can't pronounce. I want them to look different from her. I want their stories to show her she is valued for who she is more than what she does. The problem? Nobody is making that list (at least that I can find). So I'm starting one now in hopes that by the time she's old enough to pick up the lists, she'll feel wildly capable of doing great things." Hannah is three hundred women into her mission to tell stories of character over accomplishment. The honorees are nominated by the previously featured honorees. The nominations are a built-in mechanism to allow women to recognize other women for their admirable character qualities. The magazine features diverse women from every race, socioeconomic strata, sexual orientation, and professional background. Each woman is recognized for their character over their accomplishments. Hannah gets to flex her journalistic curiosity and talent for empathic listening as she personally interviews each honoree and tells their story. She leverages events and social media to elevate the stories and build a community of women supporting women in OKC. I dare say that Hannah's daughter and the daughters of many other women in the future will be impacted by Hannah's bold decision to honor the worth of women in Oklahoma City.

In a world filled with hopelessness, Hannah Schmidt's desire to impact the lives of women in Oklahoma stands out as an act of purposeful resistance. She is actively resisting the cultural narrative that someone else's light diminishes our own. Her purpose to listen well and lift up others through the graceful telling of their story is a sacred echo in a world that desperately needs to feel like their existence has a witness. As is attributed to James Keller, "A candle loses nothing by lighting another candle." When it comes to living our purpose, Hannah Schmidt stands as a luminary among us, showing us the path forward is one of being true to your design, enlivening your desires, and pressing into discouragement to find the purpose on the other side.

## Marcel Brunel

What is the opposite of life? Suicide. The opposite of family? Divorce. The opposite of a growing career? Stagnation. When I asked Marcel Brunel to explain to me the reason he is pursuing the role of emotional regulation in the field of police work, that is how he broke it down for me. In short, the men and women in uniform sign up to do good work, and the work itself crushes them. For Marcel, he knows too much to allow that suffering to persist. Disappointments in his own background and desire to see people live a full and rewarding life compel him to pursue a pathway that leads officers to healing and hope in their work and family lives.

Marcel Brunel is living proof that a life lived on purpose does not have to be a highlight reel. As discussed earlier in the book, disappointments are often the strongest fuel for a life on purpose. Marcel is the Co-founder of Dignity-Inc, LLC, a learning and development company that focuses on helping organizations see an ironclad connection between your emotions and how you show up for yourself and your team. His primary clientele are police departments nationwide. In his work, he focuses on the role of dignity to establish and maintain healthy emotional responses to the escalated work conditions in which most police officers and first responders operate. Marcel's work reveals that as officers are able to increase their personal competency in emotional regulation, they are better able to resist cynicism, pessimism, entitlement, apathy, and resignation, which can infect any frontline responder.

Marcel Brunel's personal life journey is marked by transformation and purpose, anchored by his early years in California, Ohio, and Texas, and a career that has evolved over decades. As a former U.S. Army Airborne Ranger, Marcel's path to purpose began with rigorous training and a deep commitment to service—a foundation he has carried into every role since. After studying psychology at Texas A&M, Marcel moved into sales, where he quickly excelled and found a deeper calling: helping others better navigate their emotions today and when they retire.

However, Marcel was not always as equipped to provide expert advice on this topic. In fact, his own battle with addiction and continued journey in a program of recovery better strengthened his personal attunement and interest in emotional sobriety. The root of much addiction behavior has to do with our biological reward system, namely the neurochemical dopamine. For most addicts, the path to healing has to do with learning new ways to regulate their instinctual ways of meeting their own needs. It starts with understanding that our ways of relating to reality must change. Often, this means understanding the emotional ignitors that impact our behaviors.

Marcel describes his own purpose as "helping others evolve emotionally and find the path that leads to their own emotional mastery." He came to the realization of his purpose after what he describes as his own immature responses to emotions and his addictive coping mechanisms. When he hit rock bottom and experienced the excruciating pain of despair, he decided to "stop digging." Now, he openly shares that he is a "sober alcoholic." While one might assume that he would spend his days only helping other addicts as an expression of his purpose, he also has set his sights on first responders. As Marcel walked his own healing journey, his golden repair came through his awareness and mastery of a previously undervalued aspect of himself: his emotions.

In his book *Dignity in Policing*, Brunel and his co-author outline how they engaged in successive approximations with their own emotions and identified emotional regulation as a life-saving element of first responders who consistently engage with high-stress scenarios and emotionally overwhelming public issues. They found that dignity was the prevailing emotion that was both preventative for burnout and preserving well-being. The authors write, "When we feel the emotion of dignity, it imbues us with the certainty that we are of value no matter our successes or failures. It is the one thing that we have as human beings that no one can take away from us." The emotion of dignity sounds a lot like a life lived with purpose. What is beautiful is that once Marcel was able to cultivate a life of purpose, he set out on a path to set others free to do the same. Marcel is living a life of dignity that seeks to endow that dignity upon others. He took what formerly was a rock-bottom reality and transformed into a purpose-driven leader, renewing and redeeming the stories of others.

Marcel's faith and sense of purpose are guiding lights in this work. "If you want to make God smile, go where He's crying," he says. For Marcel, God is crying for those on the front lines, like police officers, who bear heavy emotional burdens. His work with Dignity, Inc. is about building emotional resilience and fostering a life that is not merely endured but fully lived. He speaks openly about the hard truths of denial and delusion in high-stress careers, often addressing emotional topics that others avoid.

Marcel's life and work are a testament to the transformative power of empathy, resilience, and emotional intelligence. Whether partnering with city councils or advocating for emotional wellness in policing, Marcel's legacy is clear: he is a force for dignity, growth, and human connection. Through his coaching, consulting, and advocacy, Marcel invites others to do the deep, sometimes uncomfortable, work of emotional growth—to navigate their emotions not only today but throughout the journey of life. He is living his life on purpose, for a purpose.

## You

I wonder what the story could be that God is writing with your life. I imagine Him to be incredibly interested in the answer to that question. I hope you are as curious as He is excited about the answer. Where do you find yourself today? Are you ready to live your life with purpose? Are you discouraged, or have you never really explored the question? Which aspect of purpose gives you the most pause? Perhaps there is an area of your life that you need to be healed. The good news is God stands ready to renew and revive us when we find ourselves discouraged, unaware, stuck in disappointment, or in need of rest. He Himself is our very great reward.

Getting to clarity on why God placed you on the planet is a journey, not a destination. You can relax in the pursuit and lean into your relationship with God. He is much more interested in who you are becoming than in what you need to do. The truth is, He is not primarily interested in what you can do; rather, He loves you and wants for you to experience the nearness of His presence as you are going. So much clarity comes as we seek. In Matthew chapter 7, it says, "Ask and it will be given to you; seek and you will find; knock and the door will be opened to you. For everyone who asks receives, everyone who seeks finds and to the one who knocks, the door will be opened." I remember a preacher once explaining that the original language communicates this verse as a constant motion. We are to ask and keep asking. We are to seek and keep seeking. We are to knock and keep knocking. We know that God is a rewarder of those who earnestly seek Him (Hebrews 11:6). With this in mind, perhaps the clarity that we seek in our own purpose is found in the relational nature of the One who made us with a purpose for this time in history. He is not slow. He is not hiding. He is near and ready to guide.

Today, I'm calling you to a greater purpose—a purpose that may feel elusive or obstructed by past disappointments but one that's waiting to ignite your life if you embrace it with courage.

Every obstacle, every setback, every moment of uncertainty can be the very path to the purpose you're meant to live. Disappointments don't define you; they refine you. They reveal where you have been so that you can choose where you will go next. They bring into focus the depths of your resilience, sharpening the passions that pull you forward.

If you're uncertain about your direction, take heart: purpose rarely unveils itself in a single, blinding flash. It's a journey, a series of steps into the unknown, where each step shapes and strengthens who you are. Living with purpose means embracing that uncertainty, using it as fuel to search, to learn, and to press on. Your purpose is not a fixed destination; it's the pursuit, the commitment to serving something greater than yourself, no matter the cost or the path you take to get there.

Let your heart rally around this truth: You are here for a reason, equipped with unique talents, passions, and experiences that no one else has. Those gifts were given to you not to be hidden, not to be neglected, but to be unleashed with courage and conviction.

Rise above the noise, the doubt, the fear. Listen closely to the things that make you come alive. Embrace the setbacks that have shaped you, and let them propel you forward, not hold you back. Pursue your purpose with tenacity, not passivity—with boldness, not hesitation.

Today is the day to stand up, to speak your purpose into existence, and to live with unwavering vigor. The world needs your impact, your drive, and your courage. So, are you ready to step into the life only you can live?

Below, I have offered some purpose statement starter stems. I think about these as placeholders as you gain clarity on how and why God made you. Try them on and see what first pops into your mind. You can finish them on your own or turn them into questions for someone who knows you well.

*Purpose Statement Templates:*

Each of us has a purpose that calls us to serve in ways that only we can fulfill. Often, it's the moments when we feel most alive, most connected, or most driven that reveal what we're truly here to do. Take a few moments with these statements, letting each one draw out what matters most to you. Reflect on them fully, speaking honestly to the passions and contributions that only you can bring to the world.

Use these stems as a starting point and see where they lead:

"I feel most alive when I am _____ in service of _____."

"My purpose is to _____ in a way that creates lasting change in _____."

"I'm here to _____, knowing it will create a positive impact for/in _____."

"The legacy I want to leave is _____ so that others can _____."

"I'm most fulfilled when I'm _____ so that _____ becomes possible."

"The world would be a better place if I could _____ to solve the problem of _____."

"I am drawn to _____ because I know it can transform _____."

"My greatest contribution is _____, and I hope it sparks _____ in others."

"At my core, I am driven by _____, with the vision of creating _____."

"If I could devote my life to solving one problem, it would be _____ to make a difference in _____."

"The most meaningful way I can serve is by _____ to help/guide/inspire _____."

"The most satisfying legacy I could leave is to _____ so that future generations can _____."

"I know I've fulfilled my purpose when _____ results in _____."

Let these prompts invite exploration, and take your time with them. These deeper reflections can serve as guiding principles, bringing a sense of direction and significance to each day's actions.

# REFERENCES

## Chapter One: Purpose

Wilcox, Ella Wheeler. *Poems of Purpose*. Morrill, Higgins & Co., 1916. Please note this is an excerpt.

Warren, Rick. *The Purpose Driven Life: What On Earth Am I Here For?* Expanded, Zondervan, 2012.

Keyes, Corey L. M., and Jonathan Haidt, editors. *Flourishing: Positive Psychology and the Life Well-Lived*. American Psychological Association, 2002.

Csikszentmihalyi, Mihaly. *Flow: The Psychology of Optimal Experience*. Harper & Row, 1990.

Csikszentmihalyi, Mihaly. *Good Business: Leadership, Flow, and the Making of Meaning*. Viking, 2003.

Comer, John Mark. *Live No Lies: Recognize and Resist the Three Enemies That Sabotage Your Peace*. WaterBrook, 2021.

Lembke, Anna. *Dopamine Nation: Finding Balance in the Age of Indulgence*. Dutton, 2021.

Haidt, Jonathan, and Greg Lukianoff. *The Coddling of the American Mind: How Good Intentions and Bad Ideas Are Setting Up a Generation for Failure*. Penguin Press, 2018.

Wilberforce, Robert Isaac, and Samuel Wilberforce. *The Life of William Wilberforce*. 5 vols., J. Murray, 1839.

*The Gospel of Nicodemus*. Translated by George R. Smith, Early Christian Writings, 2005. Please note there are many translations.

Westminster Assembly. *The Shorter Catechism*. 1647. *Theological Seminary of Princeton*, 2016, prts.edu/wp-content/uploads/2016/12/Shorter_Catechism.pdf.

**Chapter Two: What Is Purpose?**

Keller, Helen. *The Open Door*. Doubleday, 1957.

Clements, Ron, and John Musker, directors. *The Little Mermaid*. Walt Disney Pictures, 1989.

Aristotle. *Nicomachean Ethics*. Translated by W. D. Ross, 2nd ed., Oxford University Press, 1925.

Ivanhoe, Philip J. *Confucian Moral Self-Cultivation*. Hackett Publishing, 2000.

Lifeway Research. "Americans' Views of Life's Meaning and Purpose Are Changing." *Lifeway Research*, 6 Apr. 2021, https://research.lifeway.com/2021/04/06/americans-views-of-lifes-meaning-and-purpose-are-changing/.

Kubicek, Jeremie, and Steve Cockram. *The 5 Voices: How to Communicate Effectively with Everyone You Lead*. GiANT Worldwide, 2017.

World Health Organization. *World Mental Health Report: Transforming Mental Health for All*. World Health Organization, 2022, https://www.who.int/news-room/fact-sheets/detail/mental-health-strengthening-our-response.

World Health Organization. "Mental Health: Strengthening Our Response." *World Health Organization*, 2022, https://www.

who.int/news-room/fact-sheets/detail/mental-health-strengthening-our-response.

Frankl, Viktor E. *Man's Search for Meaning: An Introduction to Logotherapy.* Beacon Press, 2006.

Science Daily. "Purposeful Living May Lead to Longer Life." *Science Daily,* 12 May 2014, https://www.sciencedaily.com/releases/2014/05/140512124308.htm.

Millay, Edna St. Vincent. *Box of Matches.* Poetry Foundation, www.poetryfoundation.org/poems/44730/box-of-matches.

## Chapter Three: Finding Purpose?

Amelia Earhart. "Quotes." *AmeliaEarhart.com,* https://www.ameliaearhart.com/quotes/. Accessed 11 Jan. 2025.

Controlling Your Dopamine For Motivation, Focus & Satisfaction. *Youtube,* uploaded by Andrew Huberman, September 27, 2021. https://www.youtube.com/watch?v=QmOF0crdyRU.

Benson, Peter L. *Sparks: How Parents Can Ignite the Hidden Strengths of Teenagers.* Jossey-Bass, 2006.

Huberman, Andrew. *Andrew Huberman - Stanford Neuroscientist & Podcast Host.* Huberman Lab, https://www.andrewhuberman.com/. Accessed 11 Feb. 2025.

Fridman, Lex. *Lex Fridman Podcast.* 2018–present, https://lexfridman.com/podcast/. Accessed 9 Dec. 2024.

Encyclopaedia Britannica. "The Science of Curiosity." *Britannica Curiosity Compass,* Encyclopaedia Britannica, Inc., https://curiosity.britannica.com/science-of-curiosity.html.

## Chapter Four: Design

Guinness, Os. *Rising to the Call: Discovering the Ultimate Purpose of Your Life*. Thomas Nelson, 2003.

Rath, Tom. *StrengthsFinder 2.0*. Gallup Press, 2007.

Briggs Myers, Isabel, et al. *MBTI Manual: A Guide to the Development and Use of the Myers-Briggs Type Indicator*. 3rd ed., Consulting Psychologists Press, 1998.

Day, Felicia. *You're Never Weird on the Internet (Almost)*. Gallery Books, 2016. And other works.

Hamilton, Duncan. *For the Glory: The Untold and Inspiring Story of Eric Liddell, Hero of Chariots of Fire*. Penguin Random House, 2017.

Wilson, Julian. *Complete Surrender: A Biography of Eric Liddell*. Authentic Media, 2012.

Comer, John Mark, host. *Rule of Life*. Practicing the Way, 2022–2025, podcasts.apple.com. While this is not the specific interview mentioned, the theme is present in his podcasts.

Rolheiser, Ron. *Failure and the Second Half of Life*. 17 Oct. 2004, ronrolheiser.com/failure-and-the-second-half-of-life/.

Loes, Harry Dixon. *This Little Light of Mine*. 1920s. Library of Congress, www.loc.gov/item/afc9999005.635/.

Williamson, Marianne. *A Return to Love: Reflections on the Principles of "A Course in Miracles."* HarperCollins, 1992.

Vujicic, Nick. *Life Without Limits: Inspiration for a Ridiculously Good Life*. Random House, 2010.

Heckerling, Amy, director. *Clueless*. Paramount Pictures, 1995.

## Chapter 5: Desires

Alger, William R. *The Solitudes of Nature and of Man.* 1865. Reprinted by Harper & Brothers, 1901. While the direct quote depends on the reprinting, the themes are present and consistent within this work.

Eldredge, John, and Brent Curtis. *The Sacred Romance: Drawing Closer to the Heart of God.* Thomas Nelson, 1997.

Cleveland Clinic. "Dopamine." *Cleveland Clinic*, 18 Oct. 2023, www.my.clevelandclinic.org/health/articles/22581-dopamine.

Brown, Brené. *Daring Greatly: How the Courage to Be Vulnerable Transforms the Way We Live, Love, Parent, and Lead.* Gotham Books, 2012.

Gabler, Neal. *Walt Disney: The Biography.* Knopf, 2006.

Saxton, Jo. *The Dream of You: Let Go of Broken Identities and Live the Life You Were Made For.* WaterBrook, 2019.

Comer, John Mark. *Practicing the Way: An Apprentice's Guide to Life with Jesus.* Publisher, 2024.

## Chapter 6: Disappointments

KonMari. "Wabi-Sabi and the Art of Kintsugi." *KonMari*, 10 Oct. 2023, www.konmari.com/wabi-sabi-and-the-art-of-kintsugi/?srsltid=AfmBOoqtmj9tLlpHVGZgYlI20Np--51ALfjoWVSKVqrshdcd0EdNIXa3.

Taylor, Steve. *Extraordinary Awakenings: When Trauma Leads to Transformation.* Inner Traditions, 2020.

Tada, Joni Eareckson, and Joe Musser. *Joni.* Zondervan, 2021.

## Chapter 7: Vision for Impact

Cooke, Graham. *A Divine Confrontation: Birth Pangs of the New Church*. Destiny Images, 1999.

Bronk, Kendall C., and William Damon. "What Makes a Purpose 'Worth Having?': A Commentary." *Human Development*, vol. 64, no. 6, 2021, pp. 446-455. doi:10.1159/000515949.

Lott, Perry James, and Walter B. Jenkins. *The Root, the Fruit, and the Dirt: Innocent Man Freed*. 2022.

Lott, Perry James. "The Root, the Fruit, and the Dirt: Innocent Man Freed." *TEDxOklahomaCity*, TED, 9 Oct. 2020, www.tedxoklahomacity.com/speakers/perry-james-lott.

## Chapter 9: Contending for Your Purpose

Roosevelt, Theodore. "Citizenship in a Republic." *Sorbonne*, 23 Apr. 1910. *Theodore Roosevelt Center*, Dickinson State University, www.theodorerooseveltcenter.org/Research/DigitalLibrary/Documnts/.

## Chapter 10: Pursuing Purpose

Oliver, Mary. *The Summer Day*. Library of Congress, Poetry & Literature, Poetry 180, Poem 133, https://www.loc.gov/programs/poetry-and-literature/poet-laureate/poet-laureate-projects/poetry-180/all-poems/item/poetry-180-133/the-summer-day/.

Erikson, Erik H. *Childhood and Society*. Norton, 1950.

## Chapter 11: Walking in Purpose

Brunel, Marcel, and Dan Newby. *Dignity in Policing: How Emotional Well-Being Saves Lives, Families, and Careers.* AMZ Marketing Hub, 2024.

www.ingramcontent.com/pod-product-compliance
Lightning Source LLC
Chambersburg PA
CBHW031529120626
46545CB00005B/2061